JUST JUNK

JUST JUNK

NEW LOOKS FOR OLD FURNITURE

Linda Barker

David & Charles

A DAVID & CHARLES BOOK

First published in the UK in 1997
Reprinted 1997 (three times), 1998 (three times)
Copyright © Linda Barker 1997

A catalogue record for this book is available from the British Library.

ISBN 0 7153 0538 7

Book design by Jane Forster

Styled photography by Lucinda Symons
Step-by-step photography by Shona Wood

and printed in Italy
by LEGO SpA

for David & Charles
Brunel House   Newton Abbot   Devon

CONTENTS

THE LIVING ROOM 29

THE KITCHEN 83

THE DINING ROOM 57

THE BEDROOM 111

INTRODUCTION

Y ou don't need to be a designer to spot a bargain and there are plenty of places to pick up real junk finds. All the pieces of furniture used in this book were uncovered in car boot sales, junk shops, charity shops and attics, with the exception of the dressing table, which was about to be thrown away.

This book has been wonderful to work on in many ways. Firstly, it has been a great challenge to make something out of what was basically very ugly, tatty and unwanted. The 'before' photographs are testimony to the disastrous pieces of furniture that found their way into my work room. It has also been stimulating to work with many different media on basic pieces of furniture. When you are considering decorating a piece of furniture, it is easy to think purely in terms of paint and various paint effects. With this book I hope to have opened up many more possibilities, such as decorating with fabric, photocopies and metal, in addition to using a range of techniques such as stamping and découpage.

When faced with the variety of projects decorated in this book it can be difficult to know where to start with your own junk finds. However, all the decorating techniques are adaptable and I hope that you will be able to find a treatment to suit your particular find. There certainly is a great deal of fun to be had from decorating your own junk furniture. Have a great time in the junk shops and car boot sales and don't be afraid to rummage around. What's more, don't forget to haggle over the price to strike the best bargain – it's all part of the fun!

Take inspiration from our 'before' photographs, and remember that even if you only manage to unearth an encrusted, sticky-backed plastic, wood-effect cabinet, you can transform it into something fantastic!

BUYING JUNK FURNITURE

First, check over your chosen item of junk thoroughly before parting with any cash; the thrill of finding a bargain dresser will quickly fade if you get it home only to discover that the woodworm was there before you. No matter how cheap the junk is, turn it over, look at the back, look inside, and even look underneath if possible. Check carefully for buckled legs, warped woodwork and blistered veneer. If you still think you can restore it, then buy it.

Practise your bargaining skills before you open your wallet. Always give the impression that the furniture 'isn't that great', and that you could either 'take it or leave it', even though in reality your heart is pounding at your good fortune of finding the most perfect piece of junk. Generally most serious traders will meet you halfway on any price negotiations, so don't be afraid to have a go.

The only items I seriously will not consider buying are those infested with woodworm. Although there are treatments available for the destruction of these little beasts, I have never felt that a piece of junk was really worth the effort. Of course, there may be a time when the junk find is too wonderful a discovery to resist, despite woodworm. It's just that I've never faced that problem yet.

Blistered veneer is another casualty that I tend to steer clear of, although if the piece is worth it, glue can be injected into the blister and pressed flat. Several heavy weights positioned over the drying glue should hold down the veneer until the surface is completely smooth again. Tiny spots of blistered veneer can sometimes be disguised with a clever paint finish or applied decoration, so there are some occasions when the problem can be resolved by a bit of cheating.

Once the ugly handles were removed, this simply proportioned cabinet was decorated with a stencilled design.

WHERE TO SHOP FOR JUNK

Charity shops are often worth a quick browse around if you're walking past. These shops have occasionally turned up a bargain for me, usually the smaller items, such as a bathroom cabinet and the odd kitchen chair. More favourite hunting grounds are well-organized car boot sales or the lesser-known garage sales. Check your local papers for details of these events and go with plenty of money, just in case it's a strictly 'cash only' occasion. It's very rare that I come away from a boot sale without some bargain.

Friends have told me of wonderful continental equivalents to the car boot sale. The summertime 'brocantes' in France are a regular occurrence in small towns and villages, and if you're on holiday in this part of Europe and have available car space, then why not make the most of the opportunity?

City street markets are also great places for bargain hunting and are usually held over the weekend. Otherwise, try your local salvage yards or auction rooms; sometimes, however, pieces from these places can be quite pricey – more antique prices than junk prices. The traders there can also be somewhat intimidating, but bargains may still be had. It is often those pieces that need more than a quick 'rub down' which are of no real interest to traders, who need to shift their stock quickly. Such items go fairly reasonably and for those who persevere it is often these pieces that may be sold quite cheaply at the end of an auction sale.

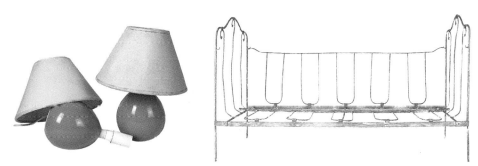

Paint and Dutch metal leaf instantly transformed two tatty lamps and a rusty old cot.

TOOLS AND MATERIALS

If you walk into any home improvement store or decorating shop, you will see a bewildering range of materials and equipment available. Don't worry – you do not need everything! In reality, you just need a basic tool kit which will provide you with all the bits and pieces needed to tackle most jobs, together with the standard colours of emulsion paints and some oil-based paints.

BRUSHES

There is a huge range of brushes available and generally you get what you pay for. I choose to work with brushes that will not deposit loose hairs all over my newly painted surface so I will not buy the cheapest ones. A good basic tool kit should have a selection of the brushes listed below.

Standard decorator's brushes in most sizes will equip you for the majority of the projects in this book. Sizes that range from 12mm (½in) up to 3in (7.5cm) will be sufficient for most furniture decorating.

Artist's brushes are invaluable for finer detailed work. Both round and flat-headed artist's brushes, in addition to a long-haired fine brush required for lining, are useful, as are short, flat-headed stencilling brushes. Fitch brushes are available from decorating shops and these are the decorator's equivalent of artist's brushes. If your art supplier isn't just around the corner, then a fitch brush would be a good alternative, the main difference being that a fitch brush is made from rather hard, stiff bristles. Fitches come in most shapes – oval, flat and angled.

BASIC TOOL KIT

Power tools are great but there is always the equivalent in a hand-powered version. I have to say, however, that I would find life very difficult without a power sander, a power drill and a power jigsaw, but it really will depend on the amount of DIY you are about to undertake. If you get hooked then you will find these tools a worthwhile investment.

Screwdrivers, both cross-head and flat-head, will be needed for practically every job. As you build up a tool kit you will find that it helps to have both a large and small version of each screwdriver, and possibly a medium size too.

A good stripping knife is essential, particularly if your penchant is for picking up really heavily painted pieces of junk. Too much paint can put dealers off buying a piece, as the labour required to strip it cancels out any profit. A wire brush is another useful tool if you plan on stripping your junk finds. It can access tiny cracks and crevices that your scraper blade cannot. An old toothbrush will suffice in some instances.

A filling knife is essential for smooth filling and repairs; look for a flexible blade and a comfortable handle.

Wire wool and sandpaper are not expensive and these items will always come in useful. It is best to have a variety of grades in both cases: coarse, medium and fine.

Glues are handy to have in a basic tool kit. PVA and wood glue are my stand-bys, while a two-part epoxy glue can be useful for really strong repairs.

Sugar soap is useful for washing down painted surfaces prior to painting, if the existing paint is not going to be removed. It removes grease and grime quickly and harshly. Protect your hands when using sugar soap, as its powerful action will be as successful on your hands as it is on furniture. Be equally careful when using strong chemicals and abrasive materials. Wear gloves at all times, and a face mask if possible. A mask is crucial when sawing medium-density fibreboard (MDF) as the tiny dust particles are suspected of being carcinogenic. Be warned.

PAINT

The enormous range of paint colours available can be overwhelming, particularly if your local paint shop has a centrifugal colour mixer. It is temptation itself to buy every specific colour needed for a particular job, whereas, in fact, the most sensible approach would be to arm yourself with a range of universal stainers, which are sold in most paint shops, and tint the colours yourself for a fraction of the cost. There has been many an occasion when a colour that I have agonized over on a paint chart looks completely different when I've opened up the can, so much so that I've often resorted to adding a drop or two of stainer in order to achieve the colour that I wanted in the first place. Many of the colours used in the book have been mixed using universal stainers, with the exception of the darker shades. I buy these colours, such as terracotta reds and ultra deep blues, specifically, but I will add stainers to them too if the colour isn't quite as expected. Do take care using stainers with darker colours, though; while tinting lighter colours is fun and economical, too much stainer can upset the balance between the emulsion medium and the colour pigment.

An acrylic primer is often used under a paint colour as a 'key' for the paint to sit on happily. Paint applied directly on a prepared wooden surface will be unstable in most instances and will quickly chip. Primer also protects the wood underneath from the paint above, forming a crucial sandwich layer.

The paint I use most frequently is emulsion and it is the easiest paint to use. Water-based colours, such as emulsion, dry quickly and it is simple to wash brushes, hands, and even faces clean afterwards. I avoid using oil(solvent)-based products as much as possible as these are harsh on skin as well as the environment. Provided furniture is well prepared and well protected using primers and waxes or varnishes, the emulsion paint will be stable, even on heavily used pieces of furniture. On rare occasions I do use oil-based products, but principally for metal projects, where emulsion paint would not work.

Proprietary water-based acrylic scumble glazes are very useful for decorative paint techniques; these dry quickly, they are non-yellowing and are simple to use. Once again, there are oil-based equivalents, but in most cases I favour the water-based glazes for the same reasons that I use emulsion paint.

Paint finishes can be used to highlight decorative carved detailing such as this table leg.

VARNISHES

There are two main varnishes – polyurethane which is oil based and acrylic which is water based. These come in three different finishes – matt, satin and gloss. Generally speaking, the higher the gloss, the tougher the finish, although all varnishes offer a good tough protection against hard knocks and scrapes. Water-based acrylic varnish is the easiest to use as it has a quick drying time and brushes are washed easily in water.

Avoid spray varnishes if at all possible; our planet is a better place without aerosols, and the inhalation of varnish particles can be unavoidable, particularly when using this product in a small, confined space. If using, always allow one coat of varnish to dry completely before applying subsequent layers.

WAX

Furniture wax, the good old-fashioned kind sold in large flat tins and smelling of rich beeswax, is valuable not only for its protective qualities but also for its decorative capabilities. The application of wax over emulsion paint gives a wonderful patina of age. It darkens the underlying colour slightly and smooths the surface, giving it a silky finish.

The wax may be applied softly with a cloth, or heavily with wire wool to create a distressed finish.

Wax can be bought in many colours, usually to tone with specific wood colours, but is more often available only in a reddish tone of brown, as well as yellow-, medium- and dark-brown tones, and clear. Always apply wax at the end of a decorative treatment as all other products will be repelled by it.

OTHER MATERIALS

There are certain specific products you will need for particular projects in this book, such as mylar (acetate sheets) for stencilling, and Dutch metal leaf used for gilding (see the individual projects). You may not have used these materials before, and it is worth keeping a list of good craft and decorating suppliers whom you can call upon for advice. Thin aluminium sheet, for example, can be difficult to find, but if the punched tin cabinet (see page 104) appeals to your sense of decoration you'll need to know a supplier. It can be impossible to have all materials at hand when you undertake a project, but knowing where to obtain specific items will save time in the long run.

Craquelure varnish produces a fine network of tiny cracks all over the surface on which it is applied. The effect is highlighted by rubbing a small amount of burnt umber oil colour over the dried varnish. The dark oil colour is held in the cracks to reveal the crazed appearance. The effect can be used in conjunction with many other decorative paint effects.

BASIC TECHNIQUES AND REPAIRS

The advice provided in this section of the book outlines the unfortunately rather time-consuming, yet fundamental, preparation techniques for getting your piece of furniture ready for its all-important transformation; it is the boring bit, if you like, as opposed to the fun part of decoration. As is the case with many decorating projects, it is this preparation which accounts for all the hard work, and decorating junk furniture is no exception. If you're not opposed to hard work, even the most severely junked piece of furniture – the sort found at the back of a charity shop or under a table at the local car boot sale – can be given new life.

Rescuing a piece of furniture that is in dire need of repair can be immensely rewarding, but be quite honest with yourself: if the thought of hours spent alone with only your paint stripper and scraper knife for company isn't exactly how you'd like to spend your well-earned weekend off, then perhaps you had better look for something that is in a slightly better condition than 'wrecked'.

SPECIAL PAINT FINISHES

Once you have completed the preparation, then you can have fun trying some of the many special paint finishes used throughout this book. Antiquing, distressing, colour-washing and gilding can all be used to give your furniture a distinctive touch and most of them are easy to do. Rather than applying just one coat of emulsion, for example, why not apply two and distress one through the other? The effect is more pleasing to the eye and it adds a strong character to a piece of furniture. A simple colourwashed effect is another easy finish and takes no time at all to apply. Colourwashing is rather like scrubbing paint onto a surface: not like painting at all, but the effect is wonderful.

There is a current taste for heavily antiqued furniture, using glazes, waxes or varnish. The simplest way to build a patina of age on a piece of furniture is to apply a coloured finishing wax; another method involves distressing the painted surface with a pad of wire wool. These finishes can be used either on their own or combined with other techniques to enhance your furniture.

Many decorative finishes are easy to produce using basic materials and a little 'know how'. A gold leaf effect is easy to reproduce using inexpensive Dutch metal leaf, while spattering, sponging and antiquing can all be created using ordinary household paint.

STRIPPING WOODEN FURNITURE

If your piece of furniture is covered with layers of old paint or varnish then it will, in almost all cases, need to be stripped. I always recommend stripping back to the wood underneath as this will give you the best possible surface to work on. The quickest and easiest way to do this is to use a proprietary paint stripper in liquid or gel form. Let your local DIY store advise you on the right product for your particular piece of furniture as there are many brands on the market. Always follow the advice given to you both by the store and by the manufacturer, whose information will be shown clearly on the label.

Always strip furniture outside if possible or at least in a well-ventilated room; the stripper can be noxious and the fumes quite overpowering. Wherever possible, choose an environmentally friendly product and make sure that you dispose of the waste according to the instructions given with the product. Wear strong household gloves and a filter mask when dealing with stripper.

Hand-stripping furniture in this way is an unpleasant task but it is often the best method of getting your junk piece back to basics. Occasionally I have taken items to be commercially dipped in huge tanks, but this is an unforgiving process as the chemicals are immensely strong and will literally strip out any life from the wood. As a result, stripped wood often cracks open and joints completely disintegrate, particularly if they were previously glued. So, if at all possible, always undertake to strip the furniture yourself, no matter how unpleasant the thought, and at least your furniture will benefit.

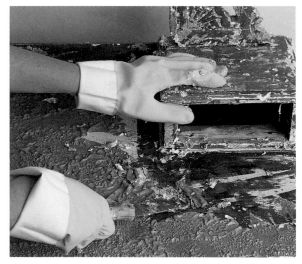

1 Decant a little stripper into a clean, dry glass jar; this is easier than tipping it directly onto the furniture from the can. Dab, rather than brush, a thick film of stripper over the painted surface, working on a small section at a time if the piece of furniture is quite large. Leave the stripper to soak into the painted surface for at least ten minutes, following the manufacturer's specific recommendations.

2 Once the recommended time is up you will notice that the paint surface has started to blister quite dramatically. The old paint layers can then be stripped away using a stripping knife, pushing the knife away from you. Scrape the old paint into a bag or container that can be disposed of once the job is finished.

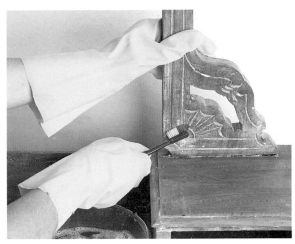

3 Once the thickest part of the paint has been removed, clean off any remaining bits using a pad of medium-grade wire wool soaked in white spirit. Rub this reasonably hard into the surface of the piece until the surface is clean. If the pad becomes clogged with paint, turn it over or replace it with a fresh pad.

4 Using a stiff-bristled small brush, brush away any paint deposits in carved details. Brush away from yourself, as the bristles may spray a fine mist of stripper and paint which would be dangerous if it came into contact with your face or eyes. Sponge over the surface with a soapy cloth to remove any remaining stripper.

5 Allow the surface of the wood to dry out a little if it still shows damp areas from the stripper. Wrap a piece of medium-grade sandpaper around a block and rub this firmly over the whole surface. This will smooth out any irregularities on the surface of the furniture and remove any small, stubborn bits of paint should there be some still remaining.

6 Wipe the surface with a clean cloth to remove the dust. Paint on a layer of white acrylic primer using a thick-bristled household brush. This will seal and protect the wood and provide a good surface for the base colour. When the layer of primer is thoroughly dry, rub over the surface lightly using a fine-grade sandpaper wrapped around a wooden block, following the grain of the wood, to create an even finish for the base coat. Smaller areas can be sanded without using a block.

PREPARING METAL SURFACES

Occasionally I have uncovered wonderful pieces of junk that are made of metal. Often these pieces are only junked because they are rusty, but as most metalwork is pretty easy to clean up I regard these finds as a kind of treat. Often the most that is needed to prepare metalwork is a thorough brush-down with a stiff wire brush. The rust will then flake off to reveal shiny metal beneath. Both the chandelier (see page 72) and the day bed (see page 50) were easily prepared in this way, prior to painting. Choose a strong wire brush and rub the metal surface with this until the rust has literally been scrubbed off. With pieces such as the chandelier and day bed you will find it easier to turn them over, working first on the underside and then on the top. Metal primer is used whenever you are applying paint to a metal surface. One coat is usually sufficient.

1 Scrub the rusty metal surface using a stiff wire brush, brushing away from you to avoid spraying yourself with fragments of rusty metal. Work systematically around the item until all the surface has been treated. Scrub the underneath surface in the same way as the top.

2 Using a narrow paintbrush, apply metal primer over the surface. I use a red metal oxide primer and it is usually sufficient to apply only one coat. Remember to apply the primer underneath the piece as well as on top. Drying times will vary, but as the primer is solvent based it will take several hours to dry even in a well ventilated space. Work outdoors if possible.

PREPARING MELAMINE SURFACES

On the whole, I try to avoid buying melamine furniture. Occasionally, however, as the bedroom cabinet shows (see page 112), the furniture may be so appealing that I'll buy it despite its melamine top. The primary concern I have with this ultra-smooth, slick surface is that it tries to resist virtually every type of paint applied to it, making it susceptible to every knock and scratch. However, a small area of melamine is workable provided it is 'keyed' thoroughly. Wipe the surface with a solution of sugar soap to remove any grease. Wear rubber gloves as sugar soap is very caustic.

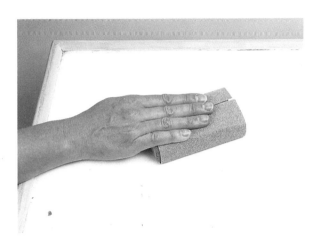

Wipe the surface dry using an absorbent cloth. Wrap medium-grade sandpaper around a wooden block and rub the block in all directions to score the plastic surface lightly, ready to receive the paint. Apply a coat of oil-based paint to the surface; this type of paint will provide the toughest finish. When the first coat has dried, a second coat or a coloured glaze coat may be applied if required; sand the first coat lightly before applying the second.

For a melamine surface that is to be decorated using mosaic, a more deeply scored surface is required for the tesserae to bond to. The best way of achieving this is to pull the teeth of a small handsaw back and forth over the surface of the melamine, quite literally gouging lines deep into the surface. This action should be done once the basic outline of the mosaic has been drawn onto the surface as the uneven, scored surface would be difficult to draw on.

REPAIRING HINGES

Often, the only action needed to repair an ill-fitting door is to tighten up the hinges, which may have become loose with general wear and tear. Hold the door firmly in its correct alignment with one hand and tighten up the screws with the other. If screws are damaged or missing, replace them with new brass ones; these should be slightly larger than the old ones so that a stronger fixing is made. When choosing a new screw, always check the furniture to see if it can accommodate the screw's length and width.

FILLING CHIPS AND CRACKS

The aim of good preparation is to have the smoothest possible finish on the furniture you are about to embark upon. When dealing with junk furniture it is unlikely that you will ever find an item that doesn't require some kind of repair, whether it is a small hole that requires filling or a deep gash across a table top.

An all-purpose wood filler solves most problems; it is easy to apply, dries quickly and can be sanded smooth so that no one would ever suspect the damage underneath. Deeper holes or gashes may require more than one application of filler.

Apply filler to a deep hole using a filling knife, allow to dry, then apply a second layer and allow this to dry. Repeat this procedure until the final layer of filler can be sanded smooth with the surface of the furniture. Use a good filling knife with a flexible blade and, if in doubt, always overfill rather than underfill any imperfections, as the dried filler can always be sanded back to a smooth finish.

Dents on the sides of furniture are better filled using a two-part wood filler, which will dry to a much tougher finish. Your local DIY store should be able to advise you on this type of product.

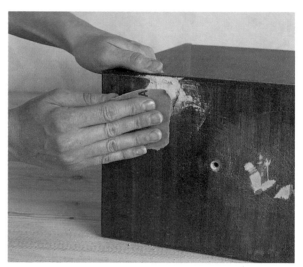

1 Apply wood filler over the blemish using a filling knife. Push the filler into the hole with the knife, using a downward motion and applying slight pressure on the knife. The aim is to push the filler deep into the gash, where it will bond to the underlying surface. Draw the filling knife slowly across the gash, pulling any excess filler with it. Apply more filler in the same way if necessary. If the hole or gash is very large, apply the filler in stages as outlined above.

2 Allow the filler to dry; it is dry when it has changed to a much lighter colour and is hard to the touch. Then sand the surface lightly using fine-grade sandpaper and gently rubbing over the surface of the filler in a light circular motion. Once the surface is smooth, wipe away any dust particles with a damp cloth.

FIXING LOOSE JOINTS

Many loose joints on junk furniture are primarily a result of heavy usage. Regluing will often rectify this type of problem quickly, and using modern glues such as PVA and strong wood glue will ensure that the joints stay closed for longer.

When regluing, always use too much rather than too little glue; any excess adhesive can soon be wiped away with a clean cloth. If access to the joint is difficult, use a small stiff-bristled artist's brush to apply glue over the damaged surfaces. After you have applied the glue, clamp the joint to secure the repair until the glue dries; in most cases, you should allow glue to dry overnight.

1 Open the joints as wide as possible without causing any more harm than is necessary to the piece of furniture. Apply glue to the joints, using the nozzle of the wood glue tube to direct the glue into the joints themselves.

2 Press the two sides together and hold firmly for a few minutes. Wipe excess glue from around the joint with a clean cloth. It may be necessary to tap the joints together lightly using a small hammer. If additional force is required to bond the two pieces back together you will need to use a larger hammer, but protect the wood from being dented by it by placing a small block of wood between the hammer and the area that is being repaired.

3 Wherever possible, apply weights or a clamp on top of newly glued joints to keep them secure until the adhesive is firmly set and has dried thoroughly. Often this will mean allowing the joints to remain like this overnight to ensure a really good repair that will stand the test of time.

CHANGING A DRAWER KNOB

It may sound basic, but it is surprising how much difference a small drawer knob can make to a piece of furniture. Recently I discovered an entire shop devoted solely to knobs! New designers are also beginning to advertise beautiful cabinet pulls, door furniture and drawer knobs in the classified adverts at the back of many design and home interest magazines, so check these pages too if you're looking for new ideas.

Remove the old drawer pull from the junk furniture using a screwdriver. If you clean away the dirt and grime that tends to collect around the screw heads on old furniture, you will usually be able to reveal the screw head sufficiently to unscrew the fixings. Rusted-in screws that steadfastly refuse to budge will either need to be cut off with a fretsaw, or sometimes drilled out.

1 Fill the holes that are left after the removal of the old drawer pull using a small amount of wood filler. Push the filler into the holes as you pull the spreader past them, and scrape away any excess from around the sides of the repair. Allow the filler to dry, then sand lightly to a smooth finish.

2 For a central fixing knob, measure across the width and depth of the drawer to determine the central position. Lightly mark the spot with a pencil cross.

3 For a central screw-fitting drawer knob, use the pencil mark as a guide for the drill. Fix a wood drilling bit into the drill, choosing a bit that is slightly smaller in diameter than the screw itself. Hold the drawer firmly with one hand and drill vertically into the drawer.

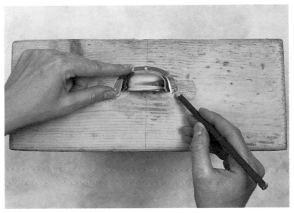

4 Screw the knob into the hole. Sometimes wooden knobs such as this one are purchased with the screw fixed in place. Other knobs require a screw to be passed through from inside the drawer, through the drilled hole and into the wooden knob.

5 For a drawer pull like this one that requires three screws, position the handle over the centre of the drawer, marking in the centre line if necessary to align the handle correctly. Using a light pencil, mark through the screw-hole positions, remove the handle and use the pencilled marks as guides for the drill.

DECORATING A DRAWER KNOB

Wooden knobs are easy to decorate; treat them as you would any blank surface. Choose unfinished wood if at all possible, as this needs no preparation at all. For wood that has been previously lacquered or waxed, simply prepare it as if it were a piece of furniture. Wire wool soaked in a little white spirit will remove wax, and sanding will 'key' an ultra-smooth surface such as lacquer. If the knobs are painted, then either sand them or use a little paint stripper.

Metal knobs can also be decorated successfully. To create an antique finish on a new brass knob, mix a little burnt umber oil colour with a little polyurethane varnish and stipple the colour over the brass surface.

Distressed colours such as bright yellow showing underneath a slate blue can be effective on a country-style piece of furniture. For the most effective results when distressing, choose colours that are opposite on the colour spectrum, as shown here.

Découpage can also be very effective on drawer knobs. Once again, choose a background colour that will set off the applied découpage. Tint the découpage using watercolours for a softer look; alternatively, a graphic look may be achieved by applying a black and white image onto a dark base colour. Glue the découpaged motif in position, then protect and seal it with at least three layers of acrylic varnish.

REPAIRING A CHAIR

Before buying or rescuing a broken chair such as this one, quickly do a test run to see if the pieces will in fact go back together. This is not as crazy as it may at first seem, as the damage may have occurred as a result of warped wood. If this is the case, the pieces will never fit back squarely and the chair is best not bought in the first place.

1 Clean the old glue from around the base of each spindle of the chair back and from the holes into which the spindles will fit. Make sure that the spindles fit inside the appropriate holes. Squeeze wood glue into the joints and around the spindle bases.

2 Push the separate parts of the chair back together and tap down using a hammer, protecting the wood with a wooden block. Bind the chair back to the base of the chair using strong string and pull the tension really tight to hold the back in place until the glue has dried.

3 Remove all the old glue from inside the joints and around the spindles of the chair legs. Apply plenty of strong wood glue into the drilled holes and around the ends of the crossbar and leg sections.

4 Push the chair leg pieces together and tap in place using a hammer, protecting the wood with a wooden block. When the joints are firmly in place, clamp the frame together to prevent any movement before the glue has dried. The easiest way to do this is to bind string around the legs, pulling the tension as tight as possible. Leave like this until the glue has set.

REPAIRING MOULDING

Intricate plaster detailing on some picture frames and furniture can become badly damaged with age and this can often deter prospective buyers. Consequently, I have often seen rather fine examples of plasterwork, particularly picture and mirror frames, stacked away at the back of junk shops. This is good news for me, as repairing plaster is not as difficult as it may at first seem. For repairing delicate moulded details, look for a specialist two-part putty which is mixed together between your fingers and built up into the missing plasterwork. This is then shaped as required to match the existing plasterwork and sanded if necessary when it is completely dry.

For less ornate details ordinary wood filler is perfectly adequate. Simply apply the filler into the missing section. You will find that the filler has enough drying time to enable you to shape it carefully to match the surrounding plasterwork.

1 Clean around the area to be filled if it looks dusty, and use an old dry toothbrush to gain access to difficult corners. Using a small modelling tool (readily available from craft shops), press a small dollop of filler into the area to be filled. Press it firmly onto the surface of the bare wood to be sure of a good contact between the wooden surface and the filler.

2 Apply more filler into the area to be filled, pressing it firmly with the modelling tool to ensure a good contact between filler and frame. Scrape away excess filler as you go along.

3 Using the pointed end of the modelling tool, 'draw in' the moulded details, matching these markings with those on either side. Keep working in this way until the desired effect is achieved and the new patch is sympathetic to the old plasterwork moulding.

SEWING TECHNIQUES

If you are handy with a sewing machine, you have the advantage where soft furnishings are concerned. It is useful to be able to replace old cushions or make new covers for chair seats as this can transform an otherwise respectable armchair. This section covers two simple sewing techniques that give a stylish finishing touch to your soft furnishings.

COVERING PIPING CORD

You can buy ready-covered piping cord, but finding a match for your chosen fabric can be difficult. Covering the cord yourself will solve the problem. Piping cord can be bought in varying thicknesses; I use size 5 or 6 for most upholstery projects. To calculate the amount needed, measure the seams and edges to be piped and add 5cm (2in).

1 To make the piping, cut several long strips from your chosen fabric, each about 5cm (2in) wide. The strips should be cut on the bias, across the grain of the fabric. Join the strips of fabric together until you have one long strip that is sufficient for your needs.

2 Fold the fabric strips around the cord and pin the edges together along the length of the cord. Baste as close to the cord as possible, then remove the pins. Place the fabric-covered cord under the presser foot of the machine and stitch close to the cord using a straight stitch. You may prefer to use a zipper foot if you have one, which will stitch closer to the cord. Trim away the excess fabric evenly so it measures 12mm (½in) from the stitching line, then remove the basting thread.

CHOOSING FABRIC

When choosing fabric for most upholstery pieces, make sure it is machine washable. For larger pieces, such as the seat base for the day bed, I would recommend washing the fabric prior to sewing, to pre-shrink the fibres. When mixing fabrics, always select those that have compatible washing recommendations and are made from the same type of fibre.

MAKING BUTTONHOLES

Buttons add a stylish final flourish to a cushion cover, and for these you will need to make buttonholes. Each one consists of two parallel rows of zigzag stitches and two ends finished with a bar tack. They can be stitched by hand or more quickly with a sewing machine. Consult your machine manual for specific instructions.

The length of the buttonhole opening should equal the diameter of the button plus its height. Test this by making a slit in a scrap piece of fabric to what you think is the right length, and then inserting the button.

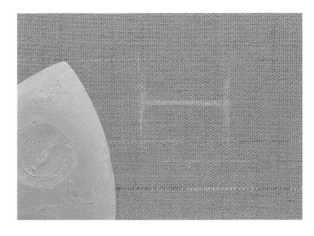

1 Using tailor's chalk, mark the position of the buttonhole on the right side of the fabric.

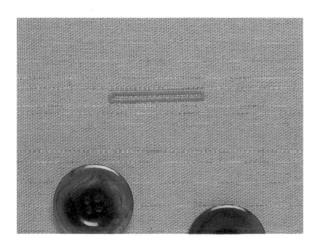

2 Stitch the buttonhole using matching or toning sewing thread. The stitched buttonhole should be 3mm (⅛in) longer than the marked buttonhole, to allow for the stitches at each end.

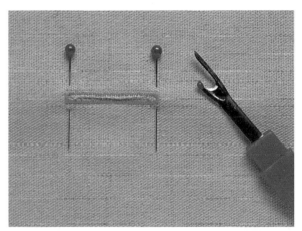

3 To make the opening, place pins at each end of the stitched buttonhole to prevent cutting through the end stitches. Using a seam ripper, carefully slit the fabric down the centre of the buttonhole stitches.

There is a huge range of colourful patterned fabric available. Be bold and go for contrasting stripes, bright checks or rich floral designs.

THE LIVING ROOM

The living room is usually the one place in the home where there is always room for a spare piece of occasional furniture, the sort that is easily found in most junk outlets. This chapter contains ideas for transforming coffee tables, chairs, a cabinet and even a day bed using simple paint effects, découpage, mosaic, and quick and easy sewing techniques.

COUNTRY STYLE ARMCHAIR

I was fortunate enough to have been given a pair of these wonderful old chairs. If you look past the tired old covers and layers of brown wax the chair shapes are strong and attractive, perfect for a complete overhaul using paint and fabric. I had stood at the bottom of a ladder as the chairs were precariously handed down to me through a loft hatch and by the time the second one had arrived their fate had already been plotted.

The chairs are wonderfully solid and quite heavy, and the only hint of decoration they had were the prettily shaped wooden slats that make up the back rest and a small amount of turned detailing underneath the arm rests. The upholstery cushions were still springy and seemed to have enough life in them, but an inspection hole cut through the upholstery fabric revealed a rather different story. The foam was breaking away at the sides and had a rather crusty-looking appearance on the outside while things looked very dark and dusty inside. All things considered, I decided it was best to replace the filling with a modern high-density foam block which can be cut accurately to size (using a paper template). Modern foam fillings also have the advantage of having undergone various safety checks required by law, and this assured safety is well worth the additional expense. Check your local press or a business directory for details of foam filling suppliers or upholsterers who will cut pieces of foam. For larger seat cushions it is best to choose a dense foam that offers more support.

As the chair has a very solid appearance with only a small amount of decorative detailing, colour distressing is an ideal treatment which, coupled with the choice of cushion fabric, creates an informal country style.

TREATMENT

Once the layers of wax and polish were stripped away (see pages 16–17), the chair was given a coat of white acrylic primer and was then ready for painting. As the chair had a solid appearance with only a small amount of decorative detailing, colour distressing seemed an ideal treatment and would give a country style finish. I decided that a bold colour would 'lift' the chair and settled on a mid-tone blue, revealing shades of pale green underneath.

For a while the choice of fabric for the covers was not so obvious; several remnants of fabric were pinned over the old covers for approval but none seemed quite right. However, an eclectic mix of several different fabrics combined together, and united only by colour and washing compatibility, seemed to work well and it was this look that was finally settled upon. Contrasting piping cord added a neat finishing touch around the edges of the boxed cover.

MATERIALS

FOR PAINTING:
- Armchair with cushion seat
- Soft green emulsion paint
- Mid-blue emulsion paint
- Wax candle
- Clear furniture wax

FOR THE CUSHIONS:
- Brown paper
- Cushion fabric
- Piping cord
- Sewing thread
- Dense foam block
- Buttons

EQUIPMENT

FOR PAINTING:
- Household paintbrush, 12mm (½in) wide
- Medium-grade sandpaper
- Medium-gauge wire wool

FOR THE CUSHION:
- Pencil
- Scissors
- Dressmaking pins
- Tape measure
- Sewing machine

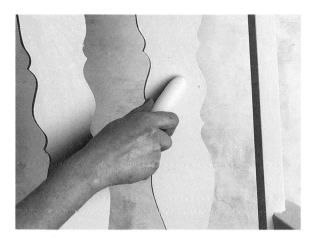

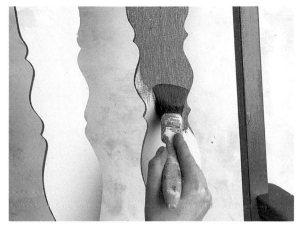

1 Apply two coats of soft green emulsion paint over the chair, allowing the first coat to dry before applying the second. When the second coat is dry, rub a candle firmly over the paint, particularly on those areas that would show more wear and tear, such as around the turned details. Wherever the candle is rubbed, the top coat will not adhere to the underlying base colour and will be easily rubbed away.

2 Using a mid-blue colour, paint over the entire surface of the chair, covering the wax completely. Turn the chair upside down to gain access to the tricky crossbars that are so easy to miss out when painting chairs. Brush the paint into the corners and the mouldings using a smaller brush if necessary, and allow the paint to dry completely.

3 Start to rub away at the top coat of paint with a piece of medium-grade sandpaper, following the natural grain of the wood. You should begin to see the underlying colour showing through. Continue to rub the colour away lightly, concentrating on the arm rests and the back supports. Use a light pressure and wear away the paint progressively rather than applying a stronger pressure for a shorter time.

4 Using a pad of medium-gauge wire wool, rub clear, soft furniture wax into the rubbed-down surface to protect the paint from further wear and tear and give it a wonderfully smooth finish. The wax and wire wool will remove more of the darker top coat, so do not be surprised to see traces of colour on the wire wool. Keep turning the pad over, and replace it once it has become too clogged up.

MAKING THE CUSHIONS

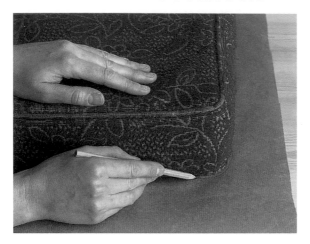

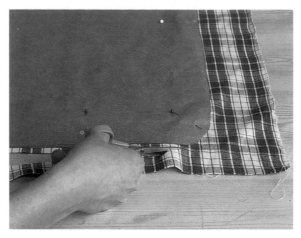

1 Place the old cushion pad on a piece of brown paper (newspaper will do if you do not have brown paper). Draw around the outline of the pad with a pencil, following the seam line as closely as possible. Cut out the resulting shape from the paper. To make sure the template is symmetrical, fold it in half and cut away any misshapen parts.

2 Pin the template onto the cushion fabric and cut out two pieces, allowing an extra 12mm (½in) all round for a seam allowance. Measure the depth of the original seat cushion and the length around the four sides. Add 2cm (¾in) to each measurement. Using these measurements, cut out a strip of fabric to make up a 'welt' for the cushion.

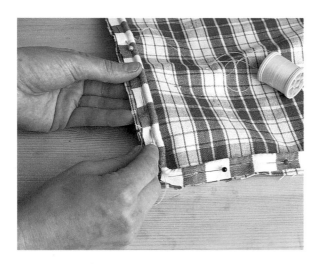

3 Pin piping cord (see page 26) around the inside of the top and bottom cushion pieces, aligning the raw edge of the piping with the raw edge of the fabric pieces. Snip almost up to the line of stitches to ease the cord around the corners. To join the ends of the cord, open up the fabric casing and unravel 2.5cm (1in) of cord. Trim the strands at slightly different lengths. Twist the strands together, then fold over the fabric strip and sew to close.

4 Pin and baste the centre welt strip onto the front and back cushion pieces using the seam allowance and ensuring that the shaped pieces are correctly aligned at both top and bottom. Sew together, leaving a large opening. Turn the cushion cover right side out through the opening and fill with a dense foam block, cut to size following the paper template drawn in step 1. Hand-stitch the opening closed.

5 To make the larger buttoned cushion for the back rest of the armchair, first cut out the required fabric piece for the cushion back. Then cut out two fabric pieces for the cushion front measuring the same width as the back; one piece should be the same length and the other piece should be one-quarter of the length of the back piece.

6 Turn under the raw edges. Stitch button-holes (see page 27) down the long side of the smaller cushion front. Pin and baste piping around the edges of the right side of the cushion back. Lay the two cushion front pieces over the cushion back, right sides together and buttonholes and piping to the inside, then stitch around the sides. Turn the cover through to the right side. Sew buttons onto the larger cushion front using strong thread. Insert the cushion pad and fasten the buttons.

7 To make the smaller cushion, cut out two cushion cover pieces and, with right sides together, stitch them together around three sides. Then turn under the two raw edges, stitching in two fabric ties to each side. Turn the cover right side out and insert the cushion pad. Tie the fabric ties to close.

DEED TABLE

A simple, unfussy table such as this one can all too easily be overlooked. My local junk dealer had had this table in his shop for weeks, and as soon as I saw it I snapped it up. The table was cheap, as to be expected in a junk shop, but not only had I got a robust, solid wooden table, but the price also included the heavy protective glass top into the bargain. The yellow linen covering the table top was quickly discarded to reveal a wonderfully smooth surface; the linen had actually protected the surface beneath. The glass, although slightly scratched, could easily be cleaned up and then replaced on the finished table to protect the surface as before.

I decided to decorate the table with photocopies of old deeds. The original source material that I had for the photocopies consisted of a number of old cheques and bills that I had purchased very inexpensively in an antique shop. Other calligraphy source material could be taken from copies of old engravings, botanical illustrations or natural history plates taken from old books. It can be worth scouring around collectors' stalls at local flea markets for examples of these. Then simply process as many photocopies from the original source as you think you may need. I gave the deed table a slightly antiqued look using cold, strong tea; coffee will have the same effect. Allow the liquid to 'pool' in some areas and remain thin in others to give a more interesting effect.

A glass top is necessary for this paper-lined table. If you aren't lucky enough to have one on the table already, you will need to have one cut, but remind the glass merchant to 'grind' the edges to prevent accidents.

TREATMENT

As the wood was in good condition, all that was required for the preparation was a good sanding down, first with medium-grade, and then with fine-grade sandpaper. I decided to decorate the table with photocopies of old deeds and cheques, the handwriting on which can often look quite beautiful. The originals are not hard to find and are relatively inexpensive. Shops that specialize in old postcards, stamps, maps and cigarette cards often uncover fine examples of old cheques or postcards with decorative hand-written details. Photocopy the handwriting and use the copies, not the originals, to work with. For an antiqued effect, you can age the photocopies using tea or coffee; simply brush a cold, strong solution of either all over the surface until the required depth of colour is reached.

MATERIALS
- Table
- Brilliant white acrylic primer
- White emulsion paint
- Photocopied deeds
- PVA glue
- Water
- 4 tea bags
- Gold Dutch metal leaf
- Acrylic gold size
- Photocopied architectural motifs
- Acrylic varnish

EQUIPMENT
- Household paintbrush, 12mm (½in) wide
- Pencil
- Sharp scissors

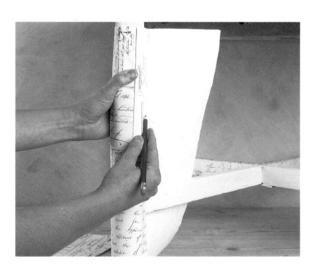

1 Paint the entire surface of the table with a coat of brilliant white acrylic primer; when dry, apply a coat of white emulsion. Leave to dry. Starting with the table legs, begin to cover the table with the photocopied deeds. First wrap a photocopy around one leg and make a pencil mark on the back of the paper where the two sides of it meet. Cut the paper to fit the leg. Try to ensure that the edges of the paper do not overlap when glued in position.

2 Dilute PVA glue with an equal quantity of water and brush a thin layer onto the table leg. Lay the photocopy over this, aligning the paper with the leg. Gently smooth out any wrinkles with your fingertips, being careful not to tear the paper. Decorate each table leg and the crossbar in the same way.

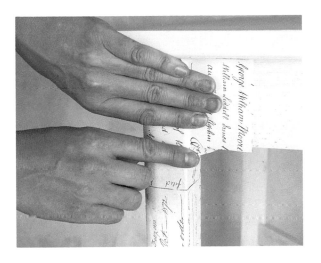

3 After the legs and crossbars have been covered, move on to the sides of the table. When gluing down the paper, wrap the ends of it underneath to keep the corners neat. Ensure that the lines of script are level, so that it reads either horizontally or vertically.

4 Cover the table top in the same way, over-lapping the paper underneath the sides. Overlap it at the corners as well, make a straight scissor cut, then glue the two flaps of paper neatly one on top of the other. Trim and discard any extra bits of paper and press down firmly.

5 Allow the glue to dry, then tint the paper with a solution of tea. Place four tea bags in a cup of hot water and leave to stand until the tea cools. Brush the cold tea patchily all over the table. Cut out squares of gold Dutch metal leaf and arrange them on the table top. Brush acrylic gold size over the areas to be gilded. When it becomes tacky to the touch, lay the gold Dutch metal leaf squares on the size, shiny side down, and gently peel off the backing paper. Distress the edges of each piece of gold by scratching it with your fingernail.

6 Cut out the architectural motifs and stick one in the centre of each piece of gold Dutch metal leaf using PVA glue. Press the edges down firmly and leave to dry. Apply two layers of acrylic varnish over the entire table to seal and protect it. If your table came with a piece of glass, replace it on the top, or have a new sheet of glass cut to fit.

STENCILLED CABINET

At first glance it would have been easy to disregard this cabinet, since its ugly handles did nothing to echo its simple proportions. However, handles are easy to remove and this cabinet immediately benefited from such action.

An attractive feature was the small pull-out leaf situated directly beneath its top. The green lino covering this leaf was in perfect condition, and I knew could be made even glossier with a little linseed oil rubbed into the surface. A pull-out leaf like this is perfect for putting cups or glasses on, thereby reducing the risk of damage to the top painted surface; once the cups or glasses are removed, the leaf is easily pushed back inside the cabinet.

Overall, the unit was in good condition, with no damage to the solid wood on either the outside or the inside. My preparation work would therefore be minimal, which is an obvious advantage when working with junk furniture. Once the handles were removed from the cupboard doors, I discovered that both of them could be opened using the narrow beaded edge running vertically at the centre. Bearing this in mind, I decided not to replace the handles on this

part of the unit as I felt that it suited a simple approach. In fact, once all the ghastly handles were removed I realized that only one small drawer knob was required, and this was to pull out the leaf. The drawer was fitted with a lock escutcheon which meant that the drawer could be pulled out using the key.

A simple unit like this one is equally at home in a living room or bedroom. With its unique, small pull-out leaf, this stencilled cabinet can be used as an occasional writing desk.

TREATMENT

I decided to decorate the cabinet using a simple, uncomplicated stencil; this stencilled design would decorate the front and sides of the unit, over a washed terracotta paint effect. The washed effect would be enhanced by applying the terracotta scumble glaze over a mid-yellow base coat; this yellow would be faintly visible through the more transparent colour, giving a soft dappled effect. This same effect can be achieved using almost any colour, providing there is a marked contrast between the base colour and the glaze. A deep golden-yellow glaze over a pale cream base, for example, would be equally successful.

There was no need for handles as the cupboard doors could be opened easily using a raised section along the door opening. The drawer was originally opened with a key, so a brass escutcheon was fitted here. The only replacement fitting that was needed was for the tiny pull-out leaf, which required a small wooden knob; I painted this to match the base colour.

MATERIALS
- Cabinet
- Pale yellow emulsion paint
- Acrylic scumble glaze (see page 12)
- Terracotta emulsion paint
- Decorative image (see page 139)
- Sheet of acetate
- Yellow ochre emulsion paint
- White emulsion paint
- Black emulsion paint
- Acrylic varnish

EQUIPMENT
- Household paintbrush, 12mm (½in) wide
- Jam jar
- Photocopier
- Cutting mat
- Masking tape
- Scalpel
- Saucer
- Stencil brush
- Spray mount

1 Paint the prepared cabinet with a coat of pale yellow emulsion paint. When dry, mix equal quantities of acrylic scumble glaze and terracotta emulsion paint together in an old jam jar, then scrub this over the top of the base colour with a household paintbrush. The brush marks should be soft and the base colour should still show through, making a soft dappled effect.

2 Photocopy the decorative image and enlarge it to fit the cabinet. Lay the photocopy down on a cutting mat, place a sheet of acetate on top and secure the layers with strips of masking tape. Cut the design out of the acetate using a sharp scalpel. Keep the edges and the corners as neat as possible, as this will make the stencil clearer.

3 Place the acetate stencil on the top drawer of the cabinet, ensuring that the centre of the stencil is directly in line with the centre of the drawer. Secure the acetate with masking tape to prevent it moving.

4 Prepare a saucer with three colours of emulsion paint: yellow ochre, white and black. Using a stencil brush, stipple the paint through the acetate stencil, laying the three colours over the top of each other to achieve a mottled effect. The finished result should be subtle and delicately blended.

5 Carefully remove the masking tape and peel back the acetate stencil to expose the stencilled image. Allow the paint to dry for a few moments before repositioning the stencil.

6 Reposition the acetate stencil over the cabinet; it should fold around corners easily if you apply a light coat of spray mount on the reverse. Apply the stencil paint in the same way as before, using the same three colours. Leave to dry. Using a clean, dry household paintbrush, paint a layer of acrylic varnish over the whole cabinet. Be careful not to brush on so much varnish that it clogs up the spaces between frame, doors and drawers. Leave to dry. Replace the cabinet handles to complete.

MOSAIC TABLE

O ne of the most appalling surfaces to decorate is melamine, so you would be forgiven for avoiding this coffee table like the plague. Under normal circumstances, I would have avoided it too; however, I was looking for a suitable surface to use for a mosaic project and this fitted the bill perfectly. Tables are ideal to decorate with mosaic as they can be treated as a flat area, like a blank canvas, and the mosaic built up like a picture.

Structurally there was nothing wrong with this table; its legs were secure and there were no chips, cracks or splits in the melamine. It also cost very little, making it an excellent junk find. Although the dark brown colour of the base – the result of a nasty brown stain – was not very attractive, once sanded and primed it would be fine for painting.

As melamine can be extremely slippery to work with, you may find that building up the sides of the table with the mosaic tiles is a little tricky. One way of solving this is to work on one side at a time, allowing the glue to set before turning the table over and working on the next side, and so on until all four sides are completed. This process might seem to be somewhat tedious and time-consuming, but it is worth it in the end.

Mosaic takes time to build up, rather like working on a difficult jigsaw, but as you see the picture starting to take shape it does become increasingly motivating.

TREATMENT

Before you can begin to decorate the table, you need to find out where you can buy mosaic sheets or tiles. Mosaic sheets can be purchased at some good tiling shops and specialist mosaic suppliers. Mosaic tiles are sold through swimming pool suppliers. Check your local telephone directory for details. Usually you will purchase tiles on paper-backed sheets; you will need to soak the tiles off the sheets prior to using them, but this is not a problem as the adhesive used is a water-based gum. Occasionally your supplier may offer a mixed assortment of tiles sold by weight. These are often sub-standard tiles but are perfectly good for this type of mosaic project. It may be that the colour is a different shade than expected or the ridges on the back of the tile are uneven; in either case this will not be detrimental to the mosaic, and the cheaper price far out-weighs any flaws. Check with your supplier first as these mixed bags are often not on display. Remember, however, that you will not be able to choose any particular colours: you take what is on offer and supplement this with sheets of mosaic.

Any surface, particularly ultra-smooth melamine, must be 'keyed' prior to the mosaic tiles being stuck down. This simply means that the tile needs a ridged surface onto which it can adhere; the tile may slide off a smooth surface. The sharp teeth on the edge of a saw are perfect for scratching a crazed surface over melamine, medium-density fibreboard (MDF) or wood (see page 19). Once the surface is prepared in this way, the mosaic tiles are laid on top of it, rather like building up a jigsaw picture.

MATERIALS

• Table
• Glass and ceramic mosaic tiles
• PVA glue
• Tile grout
• Water

EQUIPMENT

• Photocopier
• Pencil
• Paper
• Masking tape
• Carbon paper
• Hand saw
• Tile nippers
• Safety goggles
• Paint kettle
• Filler knife
• Rubber-bladed squeegee
• Cloth

1 Enlarge the lizard outline (see page 139) using a photocopier to fit your table. Alternatively, sketch your own simple motif for the mosaic. Join several sheets of paper together with masking tape. Sketch your outline onto the paper, then transfer the outline onto the table top using carbon paper.

2 Scratch the surface of the table with a hand-saw to 'key' it (see page 19). Select the coloured glass tiles you wish to use for the design, and lay these over the lizard outline to get an idea of how you would like to arrange the various colours.

3 Snip the tiles into quarters using a pair of tile nippers and wearing safety goggles for protection. Hold the tile with your thumb and forefinger and place the cutting edge of the nippers at the edge of the tile. Press the nippers together to break the tile in half, then repeat on each half to make quarters. Squeeze a line of PVA glue onto the surface of the table and lay the tiles down the spine of the lizard.

4 Build up the mosaic tiles rather as if you were filling in a jigsaw puzzle. Cut the small quarters to fit tiny gaps, keeping to the outline as closely as possible. As you work around the feet, shape the tiles to fit; in broader areas such as the body, glue quarter tiles in place without any shaping. Butt the edges of the tiles up to each other as closely as possible.

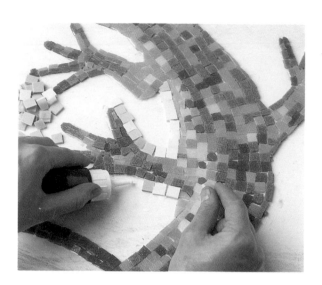

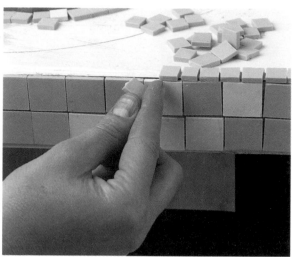

5 Glue the background tiles around the body shape of the lizard, following the contours as closely as possible. This is a traditional technique called 'opus vermiculatum', meaning literally to 'worm around the shape'. Use ceramic tiles here to contrast with the glass tiles used for the lizard and accentuate the design.

6 Glue lines of whole, unbroken tiles onto the side edges of the table (ensuring that the surface is keyed). You may need to tilt the table to prevent the tiles sliding off. Glue quarter tiles over the edge of the whole tiles along all the side edges. Ceramic tiles are used here to define the edge clearly.

7 Decorate the tiny dragonfly before filling in the background. Snip small tile quarters to shape the rounded wings and body. Glue in position. You do not need to add the opus vermiculatum around the outline as the insect is not as prominent as the lizard. By avoiding this technique the eye is automatically drawn to the lizard first and the dragonfly is secondary.

8 Fill in the rest of the background of the mosaic. Draw lines around the lizard as guidelines to follow when laying down the tiles. Try to follow the contours of the lizard's body and tail when drawing the lines.

9 Following the drawn contours, apply the glue and then the tiles, as before. Use a combination of ceramic and glass tiles to create a varied background effect. These colours were closely matched to create a sandy effect, while the variety of tiles adds a certain sense of vitality to the background.

10 Snip tiny, shaped pieces with the tile nippers to fill any gaps between larger pieces; keep nibbling away at a tile until it fits the gap as tightly as possible. There is an enormous sense of satisfaction when you fill in your last gap, so do persevere.

11 Leave the mosaic to dry overnight. Place the dry tile grout in an old paint kettle, make a well in the centre, slowly add cold water and mix to a soft dropping consistency. Spread the grout over the mosaic with a filler knife. Then, spread it more thinly using a rubber-bladed squeegee. Press downwards to make sure that all the gaps between the tiles are filled, then scrape away the excess grout.

12 Wipe the surface of the mosaic with a damp cloth to remove the excess grout. Turn the cloth over as the grout builds up on it, and rinse in cold water as and when required. Repeat this process on the sides of the table. Leave the mosaic to dry for about 24 hours, occasionally wiping the surface with a damp cloth to remove traces of the grout.

IRONWORK DAY BED

This wrought-iron bed was discovered in an architectural salvage yard, and proved to be quite a bargain. It was originally made as a children's cot, but with one side laid flat across the seat area, it is easily transformed into an occasional day bed. There are many fine examples of this type of curly wrought-iron bed, although some can command rather high prices; generally, the more ornate the ironwork the more expensive the bed.

As the side of this day bed did not cover the whole seating area, two wooden slats were laid across the gap and secured by fixing blocks, to prevent the slats moving. The base cushion was cut from a block of high-density foam. If you take the dimensions along to a specialist foam rubber retailer they will supply you with a piece of foam cut specifically to your requirements. Choose a high-density foam for the seat as this will provide a firmer base. A lightweight foam will compact easily and will not therefore provide adequate support.

Two bolster cushions provide the side support of the day bed, while inexpensive scatter cushions are propped against the metal back for comfort. The cushions are made from a contrasting tapestry fabric which works well with the fabric used to make the base cushion and the bolster pads; too much of any one fabric can overpower the effect, and using a variety adds more pattern.

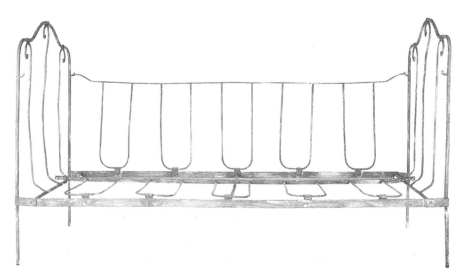

The tapestry fabric of the base cushion works well with the bronze painted frame. Buy scatter cushions in a contrasting fabric or a selection of different fabrics to prevent the whole look from becoming too stifled.

TREATMENT

The bed frame was relatively easy to prepare for painting. Small patches of rust had started to show through the old paint, so these needed a brisk rub-down with a stiff wire brush. The rest of the painted metal was also rubbed down to 'key' it ready to accept the paint. Red metal oxide primer provides a good base for a top coat of paint and prevents rust from forming again. The most time-consuming aspect of working on a bed frame like this is the fiddly painting: all the curly metalwork requires a thorough coat of red oxide. I painted the underside of the bed by turning the frame on its side. Metallic paint was applied once the primer was dry. I chose a bronze metallic paint but there is a wide range of metallic colours you can use. To cover the bolster and base cushions (the latter was cut from a block of high-density foam – see page 30) I used a rich tapestry-effect fabric, and the bolster cushions were neatly finished off with covered piping cord.

MATERIALS

FOR THE FRAME:
- Ironwork cot
- Red oxide metal primer
- Bronze metal paint
- Wood for slats
- Wood for blocks
- Wood glue
- Screws

FOR THE CUSHIONS:
- 2 bolster cushions
- Cushion fabric
- Piping cord
- Contrasting fabric for piping cord
- Sewing thread
- 4 self-cover buttons
- Shaped foam base

EQUIPMENT

FOR THE FRAME:
- Household brush, 12mm (½in) wide
- White spirit
- Saw
- Sandpaper
- Pencil
- Screwdriver
- Drill

FOR THE CUSHIONS:
- Tape measure
- Scissors
- Dressmaking pins
- Sewing machine
- Needle

DECORATING THE BED

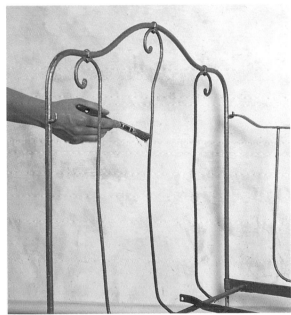

1 Apply a coat of red oxide primer over the entire frame. Do not overload your brush with paint, as this will form drips and spoil the paintwork. Turn the frame on its side to access the underside of the bed to make sure every bit is painted. Leave to dry. Clean the brush using white spirit and then apply a coat of bronze metal paint all over the frame.

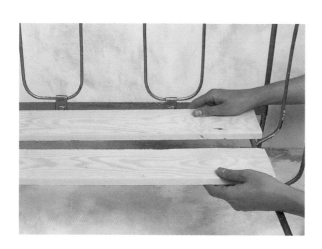

2 Saw two pieces of wood to fit the base of the frame, allowing an overlap of 2.5cm (1in) at each end. Rub the cut edges smooth with sandpaper as these will be quite ragged after sawing. Lay the wooden slats over the base to check the fit.

3 Saw four small blocks of wood, slightly narrower than the width of the slats. Lay the slats over the base and mark in pencil the point where the blocks need to be fixed. Apply wood glue on one block, then stick this onto the slat at the marked position. Screw the block in place. Repeat to attach the remaining three blocks.

MAKING THE CUSHION COVERS

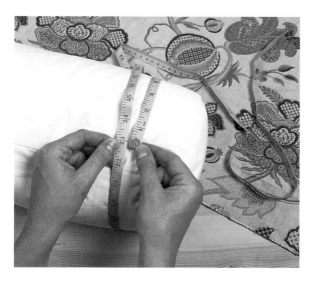

1 To make covers for the bolster cushions, measure the circumference of the cushion and add 5cm (2in) for a seam allowance. Then measure the radius and add 5cm (2in) to this. For each bolster, cut out two rectangles of fabric using these measurements. Next, measure the length of the cushion and add 5cm (2in); then measure the width (circumference) and add 5cm (2in). Cut out one piece of fabric to these measurements for each bolster.

2 Make the covered piping for the edges of the bolster cushions, in a contrasting fabric (see page 26). Pin one of the smaller rectangles to the shorter end of the larger rectangle, with right sides together and catching the piping inside the two pieces as you go. Stitch together using a zipper foot on the sewing machine. Repeat to attach the second small rectangle on the other side of the cover.

3 For each bolster cover, pin together the long edges of the bolster, ensuring that the piping is aligned. Stitch down this long edge, and you will now have a large cylinder shape. Turn the cover the right way out and fill the cover with the bolster cushion.

4 Stand the bolster on its end and gather the fabric together in small pleats, joining the pleats together in the centre. Push a pin in each pleat to hold it in place and overlap them neatly. Hand-sew the pleats in place. Repeat on the other end of the bolster cover, and on the two ends of the other bolster cushion cover.

5 Cover four buttons with the cushion fabric by wrapping the fabric over the button and securing with a few stitches on the underside, and hand-sew them onto the ends of the bolster cushions. Measure the length and width of the base of the day bed; for the base cushion you will need a block of high-density foam equal to these measurements, and about 12.5cm (5in) deep. Cover the base cushion with the same fabric (see page 34).

Decorate your finished cushions with tassels in rich tapestry colours of burgundy and gold to create a sumptuous look.

THE DINING ROOM

Dining rooms often tend towards the Spartan approach in décor, containing a table, chairs and a sideboard, and not much besides. However, this chapter demonstrates how to upgrade your dining room into the smartest room in the house, by glamorizing several dining-room accessories, and transforming a traditional sideboard.

MOCK SANDSTONE TABLE

This unusual table had some pretty carved details that unfortunately could not be seen properly because of the overpowering black wood stain covering the wood. Unfortunately, it would have been impossible to remove the wood stain completely to get back to the natural wood, because dark stains tend to saturate the porous surface of the wood too deeply. However, with a good sanding I considered the table could be painted successfully, and I purchased it with a paint effect in mind. Once the layers of stripper had removed most of the heavy build-up of wax and stainers from the table I could start the decorative effect. As the table had been heavily varnished, this meant that even after stripping, it was still very black. In order to get a good base for the light-coloured sandstone paint effect I had decided on, I applied two coats of acrylic primer to obliterate the dark colour.

When simulating a sandstone effect like this you may find it useful to look at a real piece of stone while you are working. Look at the composition of the stone and how the colours are working together, and decide which colour is predominant. I used colours that are very close in tone to achieve a soft finish. If you prefer, you could easily substitute a stronger colour at any stage of the technique.

The subtle spattered sandstone effect on this occasional table highlights the carved detailing around the edges of both the top and the leg.

TREATMENT

A delicate stone-effect paint finish seemed appropriate for this small table; the carved details on the edge of the table top and on the central support would be subtly highlighted by the technique.

The speckled stone effect is really only a sophisticated version of the spatter paintings children love to do; the difference is that in this instance the dots are spattered in a controlled manner. The delicate spray of dots was created using an old toothbrush: the brush was first dipped into thinned paint and then a finger was drawn across the stiff bristles to release the paint in a shower of tiny dots. The dots were gradually built up over a dappled paint surface until the speckly appearance of natural sandstone was reached. The amount of spatter can only be judged by eye; you need enough dots to obscure any marks left by the brush, but you also need to see enough of the underlying colour to give depth to the paint effect.

MATERIALS
- Table
- Yellow ochre emulsion paint
- White emulsion paint
- Dark ochre emulsion paint
- Moss green emulsion paint
- Water
- Acrylic varnish

EQUIPMENT
- Household paintbrush, 12mm (½in) wide
- Bowl
- Toothbrush
- Nailbrush

1 Paint the table with a coat of yellow ochre emulsion, then leave to dry. Over this, roughly scumble a layer of white emulsion paint. This involves half pushing and half dragging the paint onto the surface in a loosely circular movement. Scumbling uses the flat part of the brush as well as the tip, and allows the colour underneath to show through the brush marks.

2 When the white paint has dried, stipple a layer of dark ochre emulsion over the white. To do this, dip a dry paintbrush into a shallow pot of dark ochre paint so that just the tip of the brush is loaded with colour. Using a light, jabbing motion, dab the brush onto the table, moving the brush around so that the marks become varied.

3 Before the stippled ochre has dried, scum-ble a layer of white emulsion paint over the top, as in step 1. As the wet paints merge in together, a subtle fusion of colours will result. The overall colour will now be somewhere between white and yellow ochre.

4 Dilute moss green emulsion paint in a small bowl, in the proportion of approximately two parts paint to one part water. Dip a tooth-brush in the paint and spatter it over the table top by aiming the brush at the table top and lightly and repeatedly flicking your finger over the bristles. Keep reloading the brush and spattering the surface until the whole table is covered with tiny, soft spots of green.

5 Repeat this spattering process using dark ochre emulsion paint. Dilute the paint slightly as this makes the spattering easier. The whole paint effect should now be getting very soft and stony, with no particular colour domi nating the whole.

6 Apply slightly larger and denser speckles in white emulsion, using a nailbrush in place of a toothbrush. Use the handle of the tooth-brush to flick the bristles. Keep applying these layers of colour to the table, with white always being the final layer, until you achieve the desired effect. Allow to dry, then varnish the table to protect the surface.

GILDED LAMPS

These two lamps were undoubtedly the cheapest junk find for the book: complete with plugs and one with a working bulb, they cost less than the price of a cup of coffee. Thank heavens for car boot sales! Admittedly they did look rather shabby, but the ceramic bases were not chipped at all and I thought they would be perfect for gilding. Unfortunately the shades were not so good, and I decided it would be easier to replace these with inexpensive new ones than to renovate the old tatty fabric ones. I took a gamble on whether the lamps would in fact work or not, but at such a low price I could afford the risk. In fact, both lamps did work; all that was needed for one was a new fuse, so my purchase was well rewarded. These junk lamp bases were really quite small, but if your junk discoveries have much larger bases you might like to add more decoration to them, using the gilding as a background colour. Had I found larger globe bases I would have decorated around the gilded globe with découpage motifs. Tiny moths and insects cut from an old natural history notepad would be perfect, as it would seem that the light had attracted lots of creepy crawlies towards it. Other images that would work with equal success are butterflies, flowers or seashells. If you can find them, the Dover street publications could provide you with a wealth of material perfectly suited for découpage use. Stick the cut-outs over the metal leaf using undiluted PVA, then seal with varnish in the usual way.

These natural paper lamp-shades decorated with a simple pattern of pin pricks look most attractive with the gilded bases. Almost any design can be used to create the punched effect.

TREATMENT

I decided to gild both lamp bases; ceramic and glass are good surfaces to gild as they are so smooth. You do, however, need to apply a solvent-based gold size or polyurethane varnish, rather than a water-based size, over the ceramic base.

As I have said, I decided to replace the shades on the lamps as these were too scruffy to make good. Replacement shades are inexpensive and can be purchased in most DIY outlets and department stores. I bought some natural paper shades, which look attractive when used in conjunction with gold Dutch metal leaf, and decided to decorate them with a punched pattern, which is eaily done with a darning needle. Fabric or plastic-coated shades will not punch successfully. The punched pattern is particularly noticeable when the light is switched on, as the light shines brightly through the pattern of tiny, pin-pricked holes to create a delicate effect.

MATERIALS
- 2 ceramic lamps
- Sugar soap or strong detergent
- Red oxide metal primer
- Solvent-based gold size or polyurethane varnish
- Gold Dutch metal leaf
- Acrylic varnish
- Paper
- 2 new lampshades

EQUIPMENT
- Cloths
- Fine-grade wet-and-dry paper
- Household paintbrushes
- Photocopier
- Pencil
- Black marker pen
- Scissors
- Masking tape
- Darning needle

1 Wash the lamp bases with a mild solution of sugar soap or a strong detergent to remove grime and grease. Dry, then rub them with fine-grade wet-and-dry paper. Paint a thin layer of red oxide metal primer over the surface of each lamp base. This prepares the surface for the gold size, and acts as a warm red background colour for the gold leaf. Allow to dry.

2 Using a clean, dry paintbrush, apply a layer of gold size or polyurethane varnish to the dry surface of the lamp base. Hold the lamp carefully, using the bulb-holder as a handle. Leave the size to dry on the base until it is just tacky to the touch.

3 Place the gold Dutch metal leaf over the tacky surface, then press the backing paper down gently. The Dutch metal will immediately stick to the tacky size. Carefully peel away the backing paper.

4 Gild each base in this way. Gently brush over the gold leaf to smooth it into place and brush away any flaky fragments. Buff up the surface with a soft dry cloth, and leave to dry. Paint two layers of varnish over the gold leaf to seal. Once dry, the leaf will not tarnish, and it may be wiped clean as required.

5 Photocopy the star pattern (see page 141) to the correct size to fit your shade, or draw your own design. Go over the outlines with a black marker pen to make these stronger. Cut away the surplus paper from around the motif so that it fits inside the lampshade. Secure the motif to the inside of the shade with strips of masking tape; ensure that it is vertical and not covering a seam in the shade.

6 Begin punching the holes in the shade with a darning needle. Hold the needle firmly and rest your hand gently on the lampshade. The lines of the design will be seen more easily if the shade is replaced on the lamp and the lamp is switched on. Tilt the shade away from the bulb and do not punch the darning needle so hard that it touches the bulb. Continue to punch out the pattern around the shade.

LIMED SIDEBOARD

I found this robust piece of furniture at the back of a junk shop, covered with boxes and stacks of junk china. I loved the deep carving on the front of the cabinet and the curved centre section between the cupboard doors. Although there was a little damage to the veneer on the front of the cupboard doors, it was not substantial enough to deter me from buying it. The sideboard was so solid that it was difficult to move; it took three people to carry it from the shop to my car, which worried me slightly: how an earth was I going to get it out again? But, nevertheless, I was anxious to get started on the work because it was nothing if not a challenge.

This type of furniture is not too difficult to find, but it is better to look in the more established junk furniture stores rather than in car boot or garage sales. Because it is so heavy and solid-looking it can be difficult to sell on, so dealers will often be willing to negotiate a price. Be prepared to bargain.

I decided to decorate the sideboard with a finish of lime wax over a base colour to lighten the solidity of the piece; this effect also looks very striking. Green, grey or blue would work well as base colours, but try out a colour test first on a piece of scrap board before committing to the real thing.

Layers of heavy varnish take time to remove from an old sideboard like this; choose a fine day when you can work outside and always protect your hands when working with strong paint or varnish stripper.

TREATMENT

Preparation on the sideboard was exhaustive, but worth it in the end. Initially I used a powerful paint stripper all over it, to remove the layers of thick brown varnish that had built up over the years. When using strong chemicals such as paint stripper, try to work outdoors if the weather allows it. If this is impossible, then ensure that you have adequate ventilation in the room where you are working to reduce the build-up of fumes. Wear thick rubber gloves and a face mask if you have one.

Once the varnish had been stripped away, the surface was badly stained and marked, so I used a wood bleach to even out the wood tones and provide a good surface for the decorative treatment. Once again, this chemical preparation is caustic and dangerous to use unless the proper precautions are observed. Follow the manufacturer's guidelines and, again, wear protective rubber gloves and a face mask.

I decided on a fairly simple decorative treatment for this piece. First I painted a thinned, slate-blue emulsion over the cabinet, then I covered this with liming wax for a softer effect. The liming wax was then buffed to a sheen using a soft cloth.

MATERIALS
- Sideboard
- Caustic varnish stripper
- Vinegar
- Water
- Wood bleach
- Dark blue emulsion paint
- Liming wax

EQUIPMENT
- Rubber gloves
- Household paintbrushes, 12mm (½in) wide
- Scraper
- Stiff wire brush
- Coarse- and medium-grade wire wool
- Bowl
- Cloths
- Jam jar
- Steel ruler
- Pencil
- Drill
- Screwdriver

1 Lay the sideboard on its back or side in order to work on a flat surface. Wearing rubber gloves for protection, dab generous amounts of caustic varnish stripper over the entire varnished surface, according to the manufacturer's instructions. Allow the stripper to work on the varnish.

2 When the caustic stripper starts to work you will notice the old layers of varnish starting to bubble and blister. Leave the stripper on the surface of the cabinet for the manufacturer's recommended time. Start to scrape away the build-up of old varnish layers.

3 Keep scraping away the sludgy stripper from the surface of the wood until the surface is clear. Use a stiff wire brush to gain access to carved details and other parts that the scraper will not reach into. Work away from yourself to avoid being splattered with a shower of stripper and varnish from the brush.

4 When the sideboard is almost free of stripper, rub the entire surface with a pad of coarse-grade wire wool. Work in a circular motion to clean the surface of the wood and to get rid of the last traces of stripper. Then go over the surface with medium-grade wire wool. Mix in a bowl a solution of one part vinegar to four parts warm water. Soak a cloth in this solution, then wipe it over the sideboard. Rub the surface well, then leave to dry thoroughly.

5 Apply wood bleach over the surface of the sideboard to even up the tones of the wood. Wood bleach has two parts, both of which are irritating to the skin if your hands are not protected, so do wear long rubber gloves. Brush the first part of the bleach onto the cabinet according to the instructions on the pack.

6 When this first part is dry, brush on the second part of the bleach. Stipple the solution into the carved details, always taking care not to splash the solution towards you. Wear protective eye goggles if possible.

7 When this second part of the treatment is quite dry, it can leave a powdery white deposit on the surface of the wood. Wipe the surface clear with a mild vinegar solution; follow the manufacturer's instructions for detailed advice. Allow to dry.

8 When the surface of the sideboard is completely dry it can be decorated. Dilute dark blue emulsion paint with cold water in the proportion of two parts paint to one part water, and mix together thoroughly in an old jam jar. Brush the paint over the whole unit. Although the colour looks very dark at this stage, it will be lightened considerably with liming wax.

9 Allow the blue base coat to dry completely. Using a soft cloth, rub a generous amount of liming wax over the whole surface. Rub the wax deep into the carved details and into the recessed areas of the sideboard. Allow the porous surface to absorb as much wax as possible.

10 Buff the lime-waxed surface with a clean dry cloth to remove excess wax and create a soft sheen. Turn the cloth over as the excess wax builds up and renew the cloth if necessary. The recessed areas will hold the wax, which will enhance the limewashed effect.

11 If you intend to reposition the handles, mark the new position carefully using a steel ruler and a pencil. You will need to determine new positions for the screw fittings; mark these positions accurately on the face of the sideboard with faint pencil marks.

12 Make new screw holes with a drill. Work directly above the new position and choose the appropriate bit for the drill. The bit should be the same diameter or slightly smaller than the shaft of the screw you will be using for the tightest fixing.

13 Attach the handles to the sideboard. On this sideboard, the screws are fixed into the handle from the back of the door. Remove any pencil marks remaining on the wood by polishing with a soft cloth.

VERDIGRIS CHANDELIER

I found this beautiful metal chandelier in the back of a very tatty junk shop and coveted it immediately. It was as shabby as the shop itself and covered in a mass of cobwebs, but the spiders would just have to find another home.

The chandelier had the potential for electrification, but on closer inspection I found that the cables were badly damaged; however, I could unscrew the fittings and use the chandelier for candles. If you find a similar chandelier and are interested in electrifying the fitting, it is worth noting that some electrical shops do carry out an electrification service if required.

Although shabby, this chandelier was very ornate and the small leaf scrolls on it seemed perfect for a little gilding decoration. I tend to use the more inexpensive Dutch metal leaf as opposed to the rather expensive gold equivalent for gilding. When applying the metal leaf, allow a little of the red oxide primer to show through from underneath to simulate real gesso, which would traditionally have been used under gilding.

The arms of the chandelier and the rest of the frame were ideal for a metal paint finish. Verdigris is traditionally seen on copper or bronze and is the result of years of neglect and weathering. Here, I used a combination of bluish-green paints to simulate the effect. Because the surface is metal, it is best to use spirit-based paints rather than emulsion colours for this paint effect.

The bright greeny blue verdigris colours work very well with the antiqued gilding. This battered old chandelier started life as an unwanted, cheap junk shop find but is completely transformed with this simple paint effect and a little gilding.

TREATMENT

The condition of the chandelier was pretty good underneath all the cobwebs, and there were no old paint layers to strip away. However, the rusty metal needed a thorough rub-down, and the twisting ironwork meant that there were plenty of nooks and crannies where the rust had really taken hold.

Once prepared, the delicate, elegant leaf forms of the chandelier seemed to cry out for a touch of gold. Instead of using actual gold leaf, I tend to use Dutch metal as it gives the appearance of real gold leaf at a fraction of the cost; it would be ideal for using here. I also prefer to use metal leaf, as opposed to gold metallic paints, as it has a far superior finish and is more characteristic of real gold.

Metallic paints tend to dry to a flattish, matt finish which is dull by comparison.

By way of contrast, I thought the solid, classic lines of the iron framework would be suited to the antique look of bluish-green verdigris. Verdigris is the brightly coloured tinge that occurs naturally when untreated bronze or copper meet the elements, and is often seen on church spires. You may also see it more unwelcomely around the copper plumbing pipes in your own home. Although it takes many years to achieve naturally, with a little patience you can create something similar using paint. First the framework needs to be bronzed. Then the coloured paints are built up on top for some instant ageing.

MATERIALS

- Metal chandelier
- Red oxide metal primer
- Bronze metal paint
- Turquoise eggshell paint
- Duck-egg blue eggshell paint
- Fine white plaster of Paris or filler
- Acrylic gold size
- Gold Dutch metal leaf
- Clear polyurethane varnish
- Spray varnish

EQUIPMENT

- Medium-grade sandpaper
- Stiff wire brush
- Household paintbrushes, 12mm (½in) and 6mm (¼in) wide
- Masking tape
- White spirit
- Clean dry cloths
- Bowl
- Artist's brush

1 Unscrew and take apart the candle-holders and any other parts that you need to gain access to. Prepare the metal by rubbing it with sandpaper and a stiff wire brush. Then paint the whole chandelier with a coat of red oxide metal primer. When dry, mask the areas to be gilded with masking tape.

2 Paint the framework with bronze metal paint, taking care to avoid drips. Use this paint fairly thinly and make sure it is well mixed before starting. Keep turning the chandelier around and upside down to ensure you have painted the entire framework. Leave to dry.

3 Using a small paintbrush, stipple patches of turquoise eggshell paint over the bronze. Apply the paint sparingly using the tip of the brush. About half the area should be stippled at this stage, and the rest should remain bronze. Leave to dry; wash the brush in white spirit.

4 Stipple patches of duck-egg blue eggshell paint over the bronze and turquoise. Allow some of the bronze to show through; the result should be an even distribution of the three colours. Remember to paint the underside as the chandelier will be seen from below. Leave the paint until it is almost dry, but still tacky.

5 Press a clean dry cloth into a bowl of dry plaster of Paris or filler, and quickly dab a thin layer of the powder over the tacky surface of the paint. The effect should be quite subtle, giving just the illusion of a layer of dust. Cover the whole frame in this way.

6 Gently peel off the masking tape from the leaves. Using an artist's brush, apply a thin layer of gold size over the metal leaves. You must bear in mind that wherever the size goes, the gold leaf will stick. Leave the size until it is just tacky to the touch.

7 Lay the gold Dutch metal leaf over the tacky size, shiny side down. Press the backing paper down gently with your fingers and the metal will instantly adhere to the size. Carefully peel away the backing paper to reveal the gilded leaf. You may need a second application of the Dutch metal to cover odd cracks where it has not stuck; alternatively, you may prefer to leave some of the red oxide peeking through, as it does look very attractive.

8 Using a clean, dry brush, gently flick it over the surface of the gold to loosen any excess bits of gold leaf. At the same time the brush will press the gold down securely in place. Buff up the surface with a soft, dry cloth.

9 Seal and protect the Dutch metal leaf, but not the verdigris framework, with a coat of polyurethane varnish. Leave to dry thoroughly. Screw the fittings back into place. Lightly spray the verdigris paintwork with a tin of spray varnish. This will protect the finish and fix the dusty layer in place.

MIRROR FRAME

I was delighted to find this old frame at a car boot sale. Some of the ornate plasterwork had been knocked, and bits had dropped off, but this was repairable. A dull metal paint had been applied over the whole frame which gave the moulding a particularly uninteresting look, and I'm sure this was the reason why the frame had not been sold immediately. Junk shops and car boot or garage sales generally supply a vast selection of frames like this, and it should not be difficult to find your own bargain. Small or large, heavily moulded or simply carved, the type of frame should not matter too much as decorating techniques are usually adaptable for most frames.

The silver leaf gilding used on this frame is in fact made from sheets of aluminium rather than silver itself, which makes it more affordable. Most good art shops should be able to supply this product. The silvered effect gives a contemporary feel to an otherwise traditional mirror. If you prefer the more traditional look, however, simply replace the silver, aluminium leaf with a gold-coloured substitute. Both products are applied in the same way and both should be sealed afterwards to prevent tarnishing.

A glass merchant will cut a mirror to size if you take along the appropriate measurements. Secure the glass in the frame and back it with a piece of plywood, then tack it down securely to hold the mirror in place.

The silver effect has an antiqued look if parts of the background colour are allowed to show through the leaf. For a more traditional effect, use red gesso under a gold Dutch metal leaf.

TREATMENT

This ornate frame was perfect for gilding. However, rather than using the more familiar gold-coloured Dutch metal leaf, I decided to opt for a more contemporary look and chose to use silver leaf. This is in fact made from aluminium rather than silver, and although it is slightly more expensive than the gold Dutch metal, it is still remarkably good value. Most art suppliers will stock Dutch metal leaf and acrylic gold size.

Rather than striving to achieve a perfect covering with the silver leaf, I chose to allow the base to show through in patches. If you prefer, you could apply gold-coloured Dutch metal leaf instead of silver, but in this case it would look better if the frame was painted a deep terracotta red to simulate traditional red gesso, before gilding.

The gilded frame was varnished with clear acrylic varnish to prevent the metal leaf from tarnishing. You could use polyurethane varnish; this has a slightly yellowing effect on the metal leaf, and gently softens and ages it.

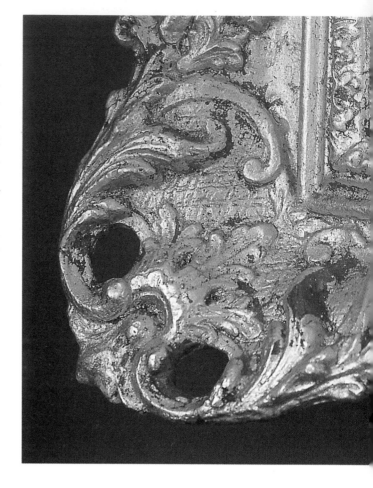

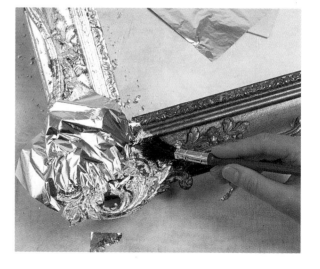

1 Clean the surface of the frame to remove any dusty or flaky patches. Using a small brush, apply a layer of acrylic gold size over the frame, working on a small area at a time. Dab the size into the details of the moulding, taking care not to get a build-up of size in the hollows. Leave the size to dry until it is slightly tacky.

2 Take one layer of silver Dutch metal leaf at a time, and lay it over the tacky size, silver side down. The leaf will bond to the sticky size on contact, enabling you to remove the backing sheet. Gently press the silver leaf into the mouldings of the frame using a dry brush.

MATERIALS

• Frame
• Acrylic gold size
• Silver Dutch metal leaf
• Acrylic varnish

EQUIPMENT

• Household paintbrushes, 12mm (½in) and 6mm (¼in) wide
• Clean soft cloth

3 Continue applying the silver leaf all around the frame. Once the size has dried the leaf will no longer stick, so work on one small area at a time. If, after you have finished gilding, there are any large areas without silver, reapply the size and then the leaf, as before. Buff up the surface with a clean soft cloth.

4 Leave the size to dry for about an hour, then apply two layers of acrylic varnish. Move the paintbrush around all the detailed moulding but, as with the layer of size, avoid a build-up of excess varnish.

THE KITCHEN

The heart of the home deserves a facelift
every now and then. This chapter does that
with its cheerful and innovative ideas for
revamping tired wooden kitchen chairs,
transforming a decrepit dresser, updating a
couple of cupboards and rescuing a tatty old
tray. To get started, all you need is paint,
paper and a sheet of aluminium.

PAINTED CHAIRS

Chairs like these can be found in almost every junk shop or boot sale across the country. The chair seen here in its dilapidated 'before' state was deemed unsaleable at a local auction and the auctioneer, who thought it was only fit for firewood, was glad to give it to me. Sadly, I think too many old chairs end in this way, although with a little basic mending they can be quickly restored. If your chair needs repair work, do this first, prior to stripping or washing down. Allow the repairs to set firmly if any wood glue has been used; several hours should be sufficient but it is preferable to leave them overnight.

Most wooden kitchen chairs like these are finished simply with polish or wax, and very little else, which makes them perfect for painting. All that is needed is a brisk rub-down using a pad of wire wool dampened with white spirit, which will soften and lift off the wax. Turn the chair upside down to access the underside. Once the polish or wax has been stripped away, leave the chair to dry out thoroughly before painting.

Almost any decorative treatment can be carried out on chairs like these; choose colours to suit your existing furniture. Often a room may suit an eclectic assortment of painted chairs, or you may choose to paint only two chairs out of a set of six; in this case paint the shabbiest chairs in the set and simply wax those remaining.

These robust kitchen chairs are perfect for a quick paint transformation. Choose a decorative treatment to suit your room and alter the colours as appropriate to your own home.

BLUE-CHECKED CHAIR

Once the repair work had been carried out on the broken chair, the decorative paint treatment could begin. All three chairs required a rather strenuous rub-down with wire wool and white spirit, to shift the years of dirt and grime that had slowly built up. As a rule, once the first layers of wax are softened and removed the task becomes much easier, so don't abandon your furniture if this initial layer proves difficult – just grit your teeth and keep going. Keep turning over the wire wool as the grime builds up on the pad, and replace the pad as required; do try to wear rubber gloves to protect your hands. You will need to work much harder around the base of the spindles at the back of the chair and around the turned detailing on the legs, as these are the areas that harbour most of the dirt and grime. The wood will start to look much cleaner as the white spirit dries from the surface.

1 Using a sharp kitchen knife, cut a piece of cellulose decorator's sponge into a square, approximately 2.5cm (1in) wide. Work on a cutting mat to protect your work surface. Paint the prepared chair with a layer of white acrylic primer and allow to dry. Then apply two further coats of matt white emulsion paint.

MATERIALS

- Wooden chair
- White acrylic primer
- Matt white emulsion paint
- Blue emulsion paint
- Coloured furniture wax

EQUIPMENT

- Sharp kitchen knife
- Cellulose decorator's sponge
- Cutting mat
- Household paintbrush, 12mm (½in) wide
- Tape measure
- Pencil
- Plate
- Eraser
- Fine artist's brush
- Medium-gauge wire wool
- Soft cloth

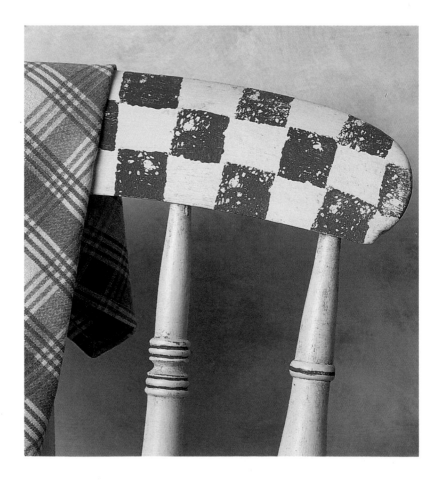

2 When the chair is dry, mark out squares on the back rest in pencil. Divide the back rest into three equal horizontal sections using a tape measure and a pencil. Start in the middle of the back rest, where the area is flattest, and draw parallel lines out to each side. Then draw vertical lines at 2.5cm (1in) intervals. Repeat to mark the seat. Dip the sponge square into a plate of blue emulsion paint, and print onto the chair in alternate squares to make a checked pattern.

3 Allow the paint to dry, then remove any visible pencil lines with an eraser. Dilute a little blue emulsion paint with water and, using a fine artist's brush, paint delicate lining details around the spindles of the chair back; any turned detailing looks effective decorated in this way. You will need a steady hand to maintain an even line; if necessary, support your painting hand at the wrist with your other hand.

4 Allow the paint to dry, then apply coloured furniture wax over the entire surface, using a pad of medium-grade wire wool. Use a circular motion to apply the wax. The wax protects the surface and gives an antiqued finish to the paint, which can be accentuated with a heavier build-up of wax in some areas.

5 Using a soft cloth, buff the waxed surface to a soft sheen. Those areas that would naturally see a build-up of darker wax should be rubbed lightly, so as not to remove too much wax. The wax will protect the chair from general knocks, spills and splashes, but subsequent coats should be applied every six months.

TARTAN CHAIR

Tartan paint effects have been enjoying a revival over the past few years, and examples can be seen on practically everything from bath towels to bone china. The colours can be tailored to suit your own requirements. Here, lime green and orange are used together for a dramatic effect, but more subtle colours, such as pale blue and slate grey, would work equally well.

Make sure there is a strong contrast between the printed squares which form the background of the tartan, and the delicate handpainted lines. A steady hand is needed to maintain even painted lines; a drawn pencil line will keep the loaded brush on the right track, but those with wobbly hands may need to tip the chair so that the back rest is lying flat on a table surface, making painting easier. It would be a good idea to have a practice run first.

MATERIALS

- Wooden chair
- Soft green emulsion paint
- Lime green emulsion paint
- Orange acrylic paint
- Acrylic varnish

EQUIPMENT

- Household paintbrushes, 12mm (½in) wide
- Tape measure
- Cellulose decorator's sponge
- Sharp kitchen knife
- Pencil
- Plate
- Straight-edged ruler (optional)
- Fine artist's brush

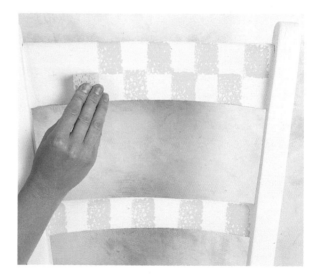

1 Paint the chair with two coats of soft green emulsion paint and leave to dry. Measure the back of the chair to determine the size of the printed squares, as outlined in step 2 of the Blue-checked Chair (see page 86). Cut a small piece of sponge according to these measurements, using a sharp kitchen knife. Plot the positions of the squares on the chair using the cut sponge as a guide, and marking with faint pencil marks.

2 Dip the sponge into a plate of lime green emulsion paint and print the colour directly onto the back of the chair using the pencil marks as guides. Do not be tempted to press the sponge down too hard as this may blur the print. The sponge will leave characteristic holes in the paint which adds to the printed character. Keep printing with the sponge to decorate the entire back rest, dipping the sponge in the paint as you need it.

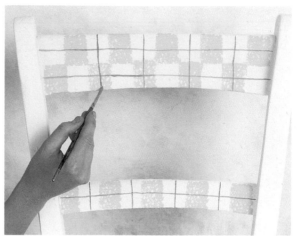

3 Once the paint is dry, lightly mark the vertical and horizontal lines that dissect the checked squares with a pencil. It is quite easy to work by eye, but use a straight-edged ruler if you think you need a guide. Mark both the long horizontals and the shorter verticals.

4 Dilute a little orange acrylic colour with some water. Using a fine artist's brush, paint along the pencil lines, holding the brush steady. Allow the paint to dry. If your chair has turned detailing on the legs, you may wish to add some fine lines here using the same colours. When dry, seal and protect the surface with a coat of acrylic varnish. Leave to dry.

DAMASK STENCILLED CHAIR

Stencilling is a quick way to add decoration to a piece of furniture, and the flat seat and back rest of a chair make perfect stencilling surfaces. If you have several chairs to choose from, the ones most suitable for stencilling are those with completely flat back rests and seats; some seats curve inwards slightly whereas others are flatter.

Stencils can be bought in almost every decorating and DIY shop, although it is not difficult to make your own stencil for very little expense. You will need transparent acetate, or mylar as it is sometimes called, which is easier to cut than the more traditional oiled manila paper; a good art supplier or craft shop should stock this. A cutting mat is convenient to use but is not absolutely essential; ordinary card, a piece of glass or an old vinyl tile are cheaper alternatives for protecting your work surface. Use a scalpel or craft knife to cut out the stencil.

MATERIALS
- Stencil motif (see page 140)
- Transparent acetate/mylar
- Wooden chair
- Soft yellow emulsion paint
- Dark ochre emulsion paint
- Yellow ochre emulsion paint
- Polyurethane varnish
- Raw umber artist's oil colour (optional)

EQUIPMENT
- Photocopier
- Masking tape
- Cutting mat
- Scalpel or craft knife
- Household paintbrushes, 12mm (½in) wide
- Stencil brush
- Plate

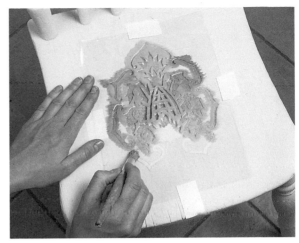

1 Photocopy the stencil motif shown on page 140 (or use your own motif) and enlarge it to the required size. Tape the photocopy onto a cutting mat and tape the transparent acetate on top of this. Starting from the centre and working outwards, cut out the darker areas of the design using a sharp scalpel or craft knife.

2 Paint the chair with two coats of soft yellow emulsion paint, allowing the first coat to dry before applying the second. When dry, position the cut stencil over the centre of the seat. Fix the acetate in place with masking tape. Using a stencil brush, stipple dark ochre and yellow ochre emulsion paint from a plate through the cut stencil, blending the colours. Practise stippling on a piece of scrap paper first.

3 Once the first motif is completed, lift up the stencil and reposition it on another part of the seat. Stipple on the paint, blending the two colours together to create an interesting effect. If the seat area is slightly curved, hold the stencil down lightly with your fingertips while stencilling, in order to maintain a good contact with the surface. Stencil the chair back rest in the same way. Allow the paint to dry.

4 Apply a coat of tough polyurethane varnish all over the chair to protect the painted surface. To enrich the colour of the chair, as shown here, tint the varnish with a small amount of raw umber artist's oil colour before applying it. Turn the chair upside down to varnish the underside. Allow to dry.

KITCHEN DRESSER

The two parts of this dresser were found in separate junk shops. The base looked very shabby and had suffered several paint treatments; the doors were hanging off and the top needed some attention. Despite these drawbacks, it seemed a good purchase: the price was low, as expected for a junk find, and there were no visible signs of woodworm or irreparable damage.

The dresser top, on the other hand, had been simply treated with one layer of a rather nasty brown varnish that would be easy to remove. The vendor seemed anxious to get rid of the top so I made him an offer and, after a little bargaining, bought it for a good price. Once the two pieces were put together they suited each other so well that I decided to treat them as one piece of furniture and make a practical dresser unit. The top was a touch wider than the base, but when hung slightly above it the difference was barely noticeable.

On the base unit, the hinges were removed and the old holes filled with wood filler. New hinges were then positioned slightly lower down and new holes were made for the screw fixings, which made the hinges much more stable. The top of the base unit needed a few carefully positioned screws to hold it securely to the frame. These were countersunk and then filled. Apart from these minor repairs nothing else needed fixing.

The finished dresser looks like a bespoke piece of furniture rather than the two pieces of unwanted junk that were bought for a pittance.

TREATMENT

Once the two unit pieces were prepared and ready for painting, I was able to look at the dresser unit as a whole. Colours for furniture will often be dictated by the décor of the room, although they should not necessarily be chosen to blend in; often a unit can look most effective if painted to stand out from other furniture. In a pale yellow kitchen, for example, this strong green dresser would look wonderfully dramatic.

The black and white artwork that I used as a design for the door panels had been sitting on my desk for rather a long time and I was determined to use it in some form or another; when I looked at the two panelled cupboard doors, it sprang immediately to mind as the proportions seemed right. In fact the designs were slightly too wide for the door panels, but I used a photocopier to elongate them to fit the proportions of the cupboard doors.

MATERIALS
- Unit top and base
- White acrylic primer
- Terracotta emulsion paint
- Dark green emulsion paint
- Photocopied motif (see page 140)
- Soft grey acrylic colour
- Black acrylic colour
- Acrylic varnish
- Cup hooks and screws

EQUIPMENT
- Household paintbrushes, 12mm (½in) wide
- Candle
- Medium-gauge wire wool
- Carbon paper
- Masking tape
- Pencil
- Artist's brushes
- Screwdriver

DECORATING THE DRESSER TOP

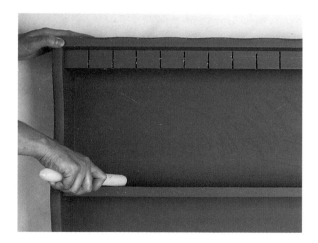

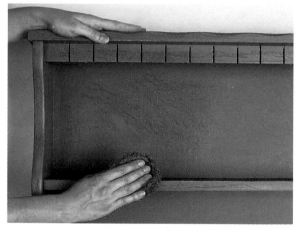

1 After stripping the old varnish from the unit, apply a coat of white acrylic primer all over, followed by a coat of terracotta emulsion paint. When dry, rub the surface with a candle. The wax will resist the next layer of emulsion paint, making it easier to rub back. Apply more wax around those areas that would naturally receive most wear and tear, such as the corners and along the front of the shelves.

2 Paint the entire unit with an even coat of dark green emulsion paint. In areas where the wax candle has been heavily worked you will find that the paint is difficult to apply. This is where the wax resists the wet emulsion. Allow the paint to dry, then fold up some wire wool into a neat pad and rub this over the surface. Those areas which had been rubbed with the wax candle will now begin to show through as red.

DECORATING THE DRESSER BASE

1 Apply a coat of white acrylic primer over the prepared base, then when dry, apply two coats of dark green emulsion paint. This base unit will have a solid colour, unlike the dresser top which has a broken-colour effect. When the paint is dry, lay a sheet of carbon paper, right side down, on the panel of one door. Lay a photocopied motif (see page 140) over this, secure with strips of masking tape, and draw around the outline of the design with a pencil.

2 Repeat this on the second door panel, to produce two identical panels. Use the carbon trace lines as a guide for painting. Fill in the solid parts of the design with soft grey acrylic colour using an artist's brush. Some parts of the carbon outline will remain unpainted; these are the shadow areas to be filled in later.

3 Once the soft grey colour is dry, tint a little black acrylic colour with the grey to make a darker tone of grey; use this to fill in the shadow areas. Use a finer artist's brush to do this, and work your way from the top of the panel downwards to avoid smudging.

4 When the acrylic colours have dried completely, varnish the whole unit. This will provide a tough, durable protective layer which will help to resist knocks, scrapes and general wear and tear. It will also provide a washable surface for easier cleaning. Replace the handles on the dresser base and screw cup hooks into the top of the dresser to complete the unit.

DECOUPAGED TRAY

You would be forgiven for not picking this tray out of a bargain box no matter how cheap the price. Yet when you see the finished tray decorated with stylish vegetable motifs and rustic paint colour, it is difficult to see why there would be any hesitation about buying it. This tray was particularly attractive because of the solid brass handles at the sides; although these were badly tarnished, a quick rub-down with brass polish would soon revitalize them.

If you are looking for a second-hand tray, always check that the handles are secure or can be repaired easily. Another obvious criterion of a good tray, although this can sometimes be overlooked, is that the base should be absolutely flat. Often trays can become warped and buckled, particularly if they are stored in damp conditions. Pick the tray up, examine it and place it on a flat surface; if there is any hint of a wobble, put it back. The plywood base of this tray was in reasonable condition; there were no splits or cracks which would have deterred

me from buying it. Always check the underside of trays for splits in the wood, as any splinters here would scratch a table surface.

I used vegetable découpage motifs to decorate this tray but you could easily substitute another image if you prefer. Select images that are printed on thick, good-quality paper, as a thinner paper may allow the print on the reverse to 'ghost' through.

The rustic, wax-distressed paint finish on the sides of this tray complement these quirky vegetable motifs taken from a copyright-free source book.

TREATMENT

Preparing the tray for painting required lots of rubbing down with a pad of wire wool and white spirit. The old layer of varnish was flaky and easy to remove in this way. If there had been several layers of varnish or lacquer it would have been easier to remove them with a more powerful paint and varnish stripper. The tray then had to be sanded lightly and the cracks and holes filled, before the decorative painting could be started.

I decided to use a simple rustic paint finish for the tray. This involved applying a top coat of emulsion over a base coat. The top layer was then worn away to allow the base colour to appear in patches. The colours used were characteristically muted: moss green and 'dirty' cream were used for the top colours, and yellow ochre was used as the base. Terracotta red or slate blue would work equally well as base colours.

The vegetable découpage motifs were taken from a copyright-free source book and enlarged on a photocopier. They were then tinted, which can be done with watercolours, acrylics, coloured emulsion paints, or even coloured crayons or pastels. As the print on photocopies can sometimes bleed, it is a good idea to seal the tinted copies with a pastel fixative; hairspray is an excellent substitute. From experience, I find it useful to cut out more copies than you think you may need, as it allows you to play around with the motifs on the tray until you are satisfied with their final arrangement.

MATERIALS

- Tray
- White acrylic primer
- Yellow ochre emulsion paint
- Moss green emulsion paint
- Cream emulsion paint
- Vegetable motifs
- Watercolour paints
- Pastel fixative or hairspray
- PVA glue
- Water
- Acrylic varnish

EQUIPMENT

- Masking tape
- Household paintbrushes, 12mm (½in) wide
- Candle
- Medium-gauge wire wool
- Photocopier
- Fine artist's brush
- Small, sharp scissors
- Pencil
- Small sponge

1 Wrap masking tape around the brass handles of the tray to protect them from the paint. Paint a layer of white acrylic primer over the entire surface of the tray, both underneath and on top. When dry, paint the tray with a coat of yellow ochre emulsion paint and leave this to dry too. Rub the top surface and the sides of the tray with a candle. Paint the sides of the tray with a coat of moss green emulsion paint. Do not worry about a perfect coverage with this colour as it will be rubbed back later. Some areas of paint will remain damp because the underlying wax prevents the paint from drying; this will be removed later.

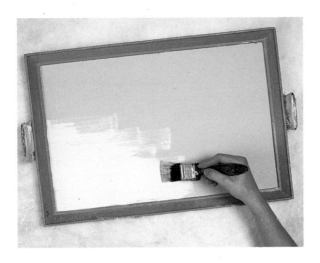

2 Apply a coat of cream emulsion paint over the base of the tray, brushing in one direction. Aim for an even coverage of paint, but don't worry if traces of the underlying colour show through as this will add to the finished effect. Allow to dry.

3 Fold under the ends of a piece of medium-gauge wire wool to make a neat pad and rub this over the surface of the tray. Rub some areas of the tray more than others, such as around the handles and at the corners, to simulate natural wear and tear.

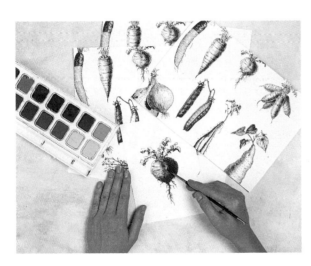

4 Photocopy a selection of vegetable motifs. Using a fine artist's brush, tint the motifs with dilute watercolour paints, allowing the underlying motif outlines to show through. When dry, seal the motifs with a coat of pastel fixative or hairspray. Carefully cut out the motifs with a pair of small, sharp scissors, following the outlines as closely as possible. Cut more motifs than you think you may need, as these will be useful when you are arranging them. Position the motifs on the tray, rearranging them until you are satisfied with the design. Mark the final position of each motif faintly in pencil.

5 Dilute a little PVA glue with a small amount of water and paste this onto the back of each tinted motif in turn. Position the motifs neatly on the surface of the tray using the pencil marks as guides. Press the motifs from the centre outwards with your finger to remove any air bubbles which would spoil the effect of the découpage. Using a small, damp sponge, wipe any excess glue from the surface of the motifs, gently blotting the area around each motif. Allow the découpage to dry overnight. Then protect and seal the surface of the tray with at least two coats of clear acrylic varnish.

STAMPED CUPBOARD

Small cupboards like this one are easy to find in most junk outlets so it makes sense to select one that is going to be easy to prepare. Had this unit been thickly painted with a heavy gloss finish, for example, I would probably have given it a cursory glance and then moved on to something else. As it was, the cupboard had been simply finished with varnish so the preparation only involved using a proprietary varnish stripper.

The cupboard had a certain appeal; its slightly bow-fronted doors were unusual and rather attractive. The lack of mouldings meant that a decorative paint treatment would not be hindered by fussy details. The condition of the unit was pretty good; there was no splitting of the veneer and the hinges were strong and secure. Another important detail was that the drawers of the cupboard glided easily on their runners.

I decided to decorate the cupboard with a stamped motif. Stamping is a recent phenomenon that can produce some wonderful results. In many ways it is easier than stencilling and can be applied to almost any surface, provided the right paint is used. Making and using your own stamping block is a great boon, particularly as printing blocks are rather expensive. This stamp is outlined at the back of the book for you to copy, but if you prefer it is possible to stamp another design.

The colourwashed paint finish is applied to the unit prior to the stamping. Almost any colour would be successful on a small unit like this; take inspiration from the rest of your kitchen.

TREATMENT

Once the unit had been stripped of its brown varnish, all that was needed was a thorough rub-down with sandpaper before the decoration could begin.

I had decided to stamp the cupboard. Stamped motifs always look better when printed over a soft dappled paint finish; here, a creamy-coloured scumble glaze was washed over a darker base coat. Almost any colour would work well on a small cupboard like this: blue, green or terracotta red would all be suitable. To make the glaze, a little of the base colour was mixed with ordinary white emulsion to make a tinted colour, then this was mixed with an equal quantity of acrylic scumble glaze. The glaze was then literally scrubbed over the base colour to build up a mottled surface.

The stamp was cut from a piece of foam and secured to the printing block with contact adhesive. You can use scraps of timber or medium-density fibreboard (MDF) for the printing block, but make sure it is at least 12mm (½in) thick so that it can be held firmly at the sides. Once the printed motifs were dry, the whole unit was protected with liming wax, which has the added benefit of lightening the paintwork.

MATERIALS

- Cabinet
- White acrylic primer
- Mid-yellow emulsion paint
- Cream emulsion paint
- Acrylic scumble glaze (see page 12)
- Stamping motif (see page 141)
- Contact adhesive
- Grey acrylic colour
- Liming wax

EQUIPMENT

- Household paintbrushes, 12mm (½in) wide
- Jam jar or paint kettle
- Photocopier
- Foam rubber
- Masking tape
- Cutting mat
- Scalpel
- Saw
- Timber/medium-density fibreboard (MDF)
- Flexible glue spreader
- Pencil and steel ruler
- Sheet of glass or flat dinner plate
- Fine-gauge wire wool
- Soft cloth
- Screwdriver

1 Paint the prepared unit first with a coat of white acrylic primer, then, when dry, with two coats of mid-yellow emulsion paint. When these, too, are dry, mix an equal quantity of cream emulsion paint and acrylic scumble glaze in an old jam jar or paint kettle. Apply the glaze over the cabinet, moving the paintbrush in a scrubbing motion to build up a cloudy, dappled coat. Photocopy the stamping motif (see page 141) and enlarge it to an appropriate size for the cabinet. Place the photocopy on a piece of foam rubber and secure it in place with strips of masking tape. Place it on a cutting mat to protect your work surface. Carefully cut around the design using a scalpel.

2 Saw a piece of timber or MDF to fit the shaped foam. Using a flexible glue spreader, spread contact adhesive on the reverse of the foam and on one surface of the wood block, and allow both surfaces to dry completely. Then place the two glued surfaces together so that they bond. Contact adhesive only works when two sides of the dry glue are bonded together.

3 When the scumble glaze is dry, mark off a panel inside each door of the cupboard using a pencil and a steel ruler. First measure the stamping block and determine the number of stamps that are to be printed in each panel. Subtract the total measurement of the blocks from the measurement of the door, and use this smaller measurement to mark out the border.

4 Brush a little grey acrylic colour onto a flat surface; I used a sheet of glass, but an old dinner plate is a good alternative. Press the stamping block evenly into the paint, then lift it up. Check that the paint has made contact with the printing surface. Before making the first print, test the block on scrap paper. Use the pencil border lines marked on the door to align the printing block. Press the stamp evenly onto the surface. Then carefully remove the block to reveal the print.

5 Reload the stamp with paint, and continue stamping, taking care to align the stamping block correctly each time. If you get an imperfect print, do not be tempted to reprint. Instead, add in any missing details by hand. When the stamped motifs are dry, rub liming wax into the surface of the cabinet to protect and enhance it. Apply the wax with a pad of fine-gauge wire wool, rubbing with a circular motion. Finally, buff the cabinet with a soft cloth, and replace the door handles.

PUNCHED TIN CABINET

This piece of junk was certainly a challenge; it was almost too ghastly to buy. However, the basic framework was sound, the shelves inside were not damaged and the hinges and door closing were fine. The revolting wood-effect, sticky-backed plastic contributed greatly to the cabinet's unsavoury appearance, but when this was removed, the piece became a perfect find that was crying out for a complete transformation.

Sticky-backed plastic coverings can be used to disguise any number of flaws on a piece of junk; it is a good idea to peel back a small section if possible to investigate the condition of the underlying surface. Upon close inspection, the door proved to be fine with no visible damage at all. The grooves chanelled across it would ordinarily have caused more of a problem, but as the front of the cabinet was going to be covered in tin, there was no difficulty.

A cabinet such as this one would usually be used in a bathroom as a medicine cabinet. However, when decorated with a punched tin effect it is equally suitable in a kitchen, where it can be used for storing herbs and spices.

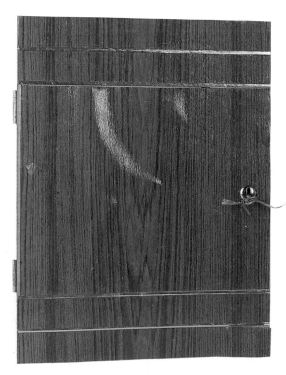

I used a bird motif for the punched tin design, but other designs can be substituted as you wish. Floral shapes work well, as do geometric patterns and strong heart shapes. Draw out your image on a piece of paper first, before committing yourself to the real thing.

This old bathroom cabinet has not only been given a new lease of life, it has also switched roles; no longer used for bathroom bottles and medicines, the cabinet is now used for herb and spice storage.

6 Spread contact adhesive liberally over the front of the cabinet door using a rubber-bladed grout spreader or a homemade cardboard spreader. Then spread the adhesive on the wrong side of the punched tin panel in the same way. Allow both surfaces to dry.

7 Once the glued surfaces are dry, align them carefully, then press them together. Make sure that your alignment is accurate, as once the adhesive surfaces touch they will be difficult to separate. Leave the adhesive to bond for several hours with some heavy books piled on top.

8 When the adhesive has set firmly, hammer in a few tacks along the outer punched edge. If your tacks are slightly too long and the ends push through to the other side, cut them off with a hacksaw.

9 Screw a small chrome knob or handle to the front of the cabinet to open and close the door. If you have difficulty finding an appropriate knob, simply spray or gild your own with silver Dutch metal leaf; if you do this, remember to seal it with polyurethane varnish before fixing it to the cabinet.

THE BEDROOM

Bedroom furniture is readily available from many junk outlets. Battered blanket boxes, chipped chests of drawers and dented dressing tables are all easily found. In this chapter there are plenty of creative ideas for improving shabby junk furniture using techniques such as stencilling, découpage, antiquing and simple handpainting.

ANTIQUED CABINET

This attractive cabinet was quite a bargain in a local junk shop and was simply varnished so I knew there was little preparation to be done. I didn't worry about the dreadful handles or the formica top as these could both be changed very easily. Replacement handles are inexpensive and can greatly alter the character of a piece of furniture. Likewise, formica is easy to paint once the surface has been washed with sugar soap and 'keyed' lightly with abrasive paper. I particularly liked the simple moulding around each of the door panels on the cabinet, which could become an important feature in certain decorating schemes, especially the one I had planned.

I had decided to decorate the cabinet with découpage and an antiqued, crackle-glazed finish. The découpage cut-outs can be taken from almost any source. I generally use black and white images that I then colour softly with watercolours. Coloured prints tend to be heavy and the print tones too strong for the design to work effectively. Use photocopies to preserve the original prints and use the enlargement facility to scale up the motif according to your piece of furniture. If you use images taken from greetings cards that are printed on thick card, you will need to peel off some of the cardboard layers before gluing down the images. Thick card will need many layers of varnish applied to get rid of the ridges around the cut-outs; by thinning the card first you will save time later on.

The simple moulded details on this bedroom cabinet frame the delicately coloured découpage cut-outs perfectly, while the fine cracks of the glaze add to the subtle decorative effect.

TREATMENT

I decided to decorate this bedroom cabinet with tinted, découpage cut-outs and an antiqued finish using a crackle varnish, which gives a fine network of cracks over the surface of the cabinet. The crazed appearance occurs when the faster-drying varnish is applied over the slower-drying base varnish. As the cracks are very fine, it is only when they are highlighted with artist's oil colour that the true effect is seen.

A pale green base coat was chosen to show the crackle effect to its best advantage. The application of both the varnish and the oil paint will darken the base colour considerably. The motif chosen for the applied decoration was taken from a black and white copyright-free source book.

MATERIALS

- Cabinet
- White acrylic primer
- Pale yellow emulsion paint
- Découpage images
- Watercolour or gouache paints
- Pastel fixative or hairspray
- PVA glue
- Water
- Two-part water-based crackle glaze
- Raw umber artist's oil colour
- White spirit
- Polyurethane varnish

EQUIPMENT

- Household paintbrushes, 12mm (½in) wide
- Photocopier
- Fine artist's brush
- Small, sharp scissors
- Sponge
- Soft cloths
- Steel ruler
- Pencil

1 Paint the sides of the cupboard, first with white acrylic primer and then with two coats of pale yellow emulsion paint, allowing each coat to dry before applying the next. Select your découpage images and photocopy them to the correct size to fit on the cabinet. Using an artist's brush, tint the images with dilute watercolour or gouache paints until you have the right tone. The colours should be muted; test them out on a piece of scrap paper first. When the paint has dried, seal the photocopies with pastel fixative or hairspray. Cut out the tinted photocopies using a pair of small, sharp scissors.

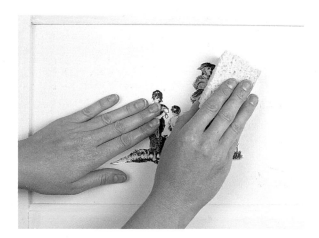

2 Dilute PVA glue in the proportion of one part water to one part glue. Paste the images with this dilute glue, and stick them in position on the cabinet, making sure that the edges are stuck down. Using a damp sponge, dab over the surface of the découpage to remove air bubbles and any excess glue.

3 Apply two-part water-based crackle glaze over the cupboard to produce a delicate cracked finish when dry. Brush on the first part of the varnish using a clean, dry household paintbrush; apply it smoothly and thinly and leave to dry. When the surface is dry, apply the second part of the crackle varnish, again using a clean, dry brush. Apply the varnish as thinly as possible, then leave to dry.

4 When the varnish is completely dry, tiny delicate cracks will have appeared all over the surface. Using a soft cloth, rub raw umber artist's oil colour over the surface of the crackle varnish to highlight the fine cracks.

5 Rub off the excess oil colour with a clean cloth; the dark colour will remain in the cracks. If there are some areas where there is too much oil colour and it looks too dark, use a little white spirit on your cloth to rub it off. The effect should be one of aged cracks; the furniture should not look 'muddy' or gloomy.

6 Key the formica surface with sandpaper (see page 19). Apply a coat of pale yellow emulsion paint. Leave to dry. Using a ruler, mark a narrow border around the edge: make small pencil marks 2.5cm (1in) from the outer edge, then join them with a pencil line, using a steel ruler. Using a fine artist's brush and raw umber artist's oil colour, paint along the pencil line. Keep the brush evenly loaded with paint to ensure that the line retains a regular thickness. When dry, varnish with polyurethane varnish.

DRESSING-TABLE SET

Mismatched wooden dressing-table pieces like these can be found in many places and assembled together for a unifying treatment. Here, small candlesticks, a wooden box and a hand mirror are all treated in a similar way and they work together perfectly. Other items you could look for could include jewellery boxes and hairbrushes, although the latter should be well scrubbed prior to decorating. The rich plum base colour here was chosen to work with an existing bedroom scheme. Choose your own background colour according to your own particular scheme or simply choose a colour that appeals. The only colours that should really be avoided are those that are close to that of the paper cut-outs, as the effect will not be as noticeable.

Any shape of paper cut-out may be applied over the surface of your junk items. These curly arabesque shapes were inspired by fretwork panels in my own home but sources can come from anywhere. Printed patterns on fabric or clothes, or patterns from nature could provide the inspiration. Draw your designs onto a piece of paper first and shade in the solid areas to gauge for yourself how the final effect will look. Once you are satisfied, you can use this as a template for your design. The fine painted line around the edge of each item gives a neat, crisp finish. Alter this colour accordingly to match the colour of your paper cut-outs.

Group together an assortment of mismatched items that would not be out of place on a dressing table. Unify these items with a simple, decorative treatment such as this unique paper cut-out technique.

TREATMENT

These accessories were painted with deep plum-coloured emulsion, and then decorated with creamy parchment paper cut-outs. Other colours can be selected to match specific decorating schemes, but a deeper colour provides a contrast to the paler paper cut-outs. Both deep crimson red or royal blue would be suitably dramatic and bold.

The paper cut-outs are delicate to handle. I found that it is easier if you apply adhesive to the wooden surface rather than to the paper itself. A successful trick is to dip your forefinger into cold water and rub this over the surface of the freshly applied glue; the glue then becomes quite soft, and you will be able to slide the cut-out over this surface until it is in the right place.

1 Paint the dressing-table items with deep plum emulsion paint and leave to dry. Place the mirror on the parchment paper and draw around the edge with a pencil. Repeat with each dressing-table item.

MATERIALS

- Dressing-table items
- Deep plum emulsion paint
- Semi-transparent parchment paper
- PVA glue
- Water
- Yellow ochre emulsion paint
- Acrylic varnish

EQUIPMENT

- Household paintbrushes, 12mm (½in) and 6mm (¼in) wide
- Pencil
- Photocopier
- Cutting mat
- Masking tape
- Scalpel
- Sponge
- Fine artist's brush

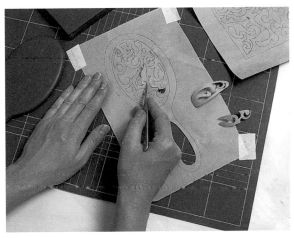

2 Draw a second line approximately 12mm (½in) in from the previous line, to mark the area that the paper cut-out will fill. Draw a decorative design in this central area, either freehand or photocopy the image on page 140 and transfer it to the paper. Repeat with each item.

3 Lay the parchment paper on a cutting mat and secure with strips of masking tape. Using a sharp scalpel, cut out the decorative image very accurately. Turn the blade smoothly around the corners, keeping the edges sharp.

4 Apply PVA glue to the back of the mirror, then stick the paper cut-out in position (see Treatment, above). Tap down the cut-out gently to avoid trapping any air bubbles beneath the paper which will spoil the effect. Decorate each dressing-table item in the same way. Dip a clean sponge in water and gently wipe the surface of each cut-out to remove any excess glue. Take care not to dislodge the paper; start off by dabbing downwards, and pressing the cut-out firmly in place. Leave to dry.

5 Paint a fine line on each of the objects using a fine artist's brush and yellow ochre paint, keeping the line smooth and even. Line the detailing on the turned candlesticks, resting your painting hand on the table and turning the candlestick with your free hand. In the same way, paint a fine line between the cut-out image and the edge of each object. Paint acrylic varnish over the cut-out, leaving one coat to dry thoroughly before applying the next. Apply as many layers of varnish as are necessary to smooth out the paper ridges.

BLANKET BOX

This type of wooden blanket box should not be difficult to find in your local junk shop or garage sale. In particular, look out for those boxes with flat sides that have no extra moulded decoration, as these will make it easier to create an interesting print-room effect, the style of decoration I had decided on for this old blanket box.

There is a growing interest in the 'print-room style' and you will find no shortage of suppliers of print material. Copyright-free source books are excellent for reproduction prints and borders. In addition to these, some antique and junk fairs have boxes of old prints and engravings that are simple to photocopy. Start to collect an imaginative mixture of prints, perhaps limiting your collection to a single subject or theme, such as architectural or historical buildings. Animal engravings, such as those used here, can create an individual look; botanical images are also easy to source and can look stunning. Black and white images work best; these should be photocopied to preserve the originals. Using a photocopier has the added benefit of allowing you to enlarge or sometimes reduce the original to suit your overall design. Other colours that are successful for this 'print-room style' are strong sunny yellows, Wedgwood blue or creamy 'off' whites.

Use the blanket box for storing bedroom linens and fabrics or, perhaps more usefully, to resolve the storage problem of books, magazines or tapes.

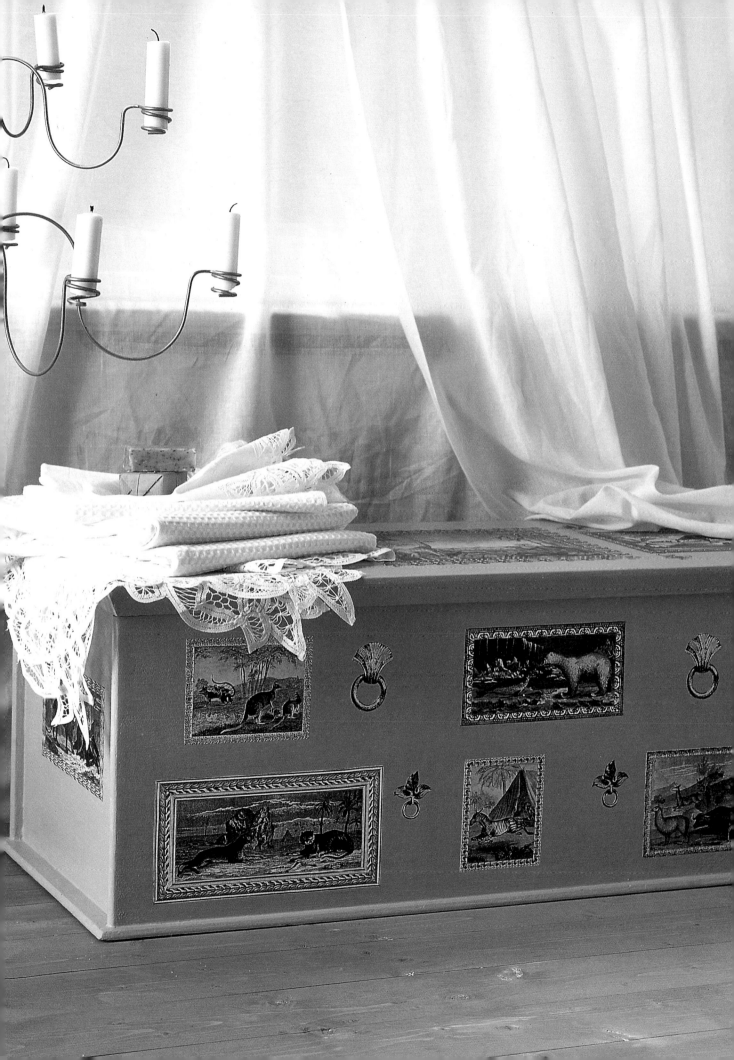

TREATMENT

After preparing the blanket box, I painted it with a coat of traditional duck-egg blue paint; if you prefer, you could use rich sunny yellows or deep terracotta reds equally successfully. I then decorated the box with the printed photocopied material, which was glued on in selected positions using diluted PVA glue.

Select and assemble all your prints and borders before starting to cut; it is a good idea to make sure that you have an excess of prints, as you invariably end up using more than you expected. Cut out the prints carefully with small sharp scissors and position these onto the box using tabs of adhesive putty where necessary. Next, cut out the photocopied borders. This part of creating the print-room style is usually the most time-consuming. Often the borders are scalloped or delicately shaped, and care should be taken to cut these out neatly. The easiest way to start positioning the prints is to place the largest one in a central position first and then to add the smaller ones around this. Then add the scalloped frames, and lastly the bows or other decorative flourishes.

Some print-room styles benefit from being given an antiqued look. One way to do this is simply to make a cup of strong tea, allow it to cool, then brush the cold tea over the surface of the prints. Be careful not to saturate the paper; a little tea will work instantly.

MATERIALS

- Blanket box
- Duck-egg blue traditional paint
- Découpage motifs
- PVA glue
- Water
- Matt acrylic varnish

EQUIPMENT

- Household paint-brush, 12mm (½in) wide
- Photocopier
- Pencil
- Small, sharp scissors
- Tape measure (optional)
- Sponge
- Steel ruler
- Scalpel

1 Paint the entire blanket box with a coat of duck-egg blue traditional paint, and leave to dry. Select your motifs to decorate the box and photocopy them, increasing the size wherever necessary. I used animal illustrations for the main images and a border print for the framing. Arrange the photocopied images on the box, then mark these positions with faint pencil marks. Vary the sizes of the prints for interest.

2 Cut out all the images and frames using a pair of small, sharp scissors. It is worth spending time doing this neatly, because the more detail you cut out of the framing and decorative pieces, the more effective the whole box will look in the end. Make sure you have enough framing pieces to go around all the images you will be using.

3 Dilute PVA glue in the proportion of one part glue to one part water. Brush this glue over the back of each motif in turn, then stick them onto the front of the box using the pencil marks as a guide. Ensure that the images are square with the edges of the box and aligned with each other. Use a tape measure if you are unsure. Wipe off any excess glue with a damp sponge, rolling it towards the edges to remove any air bubbles.

4 Glue down the framing pieces. To achieve neat mitred edges, glue the two strips of framing in place so that they overlap at the corners. While the glue is damp, place a steel ruler over each corner in turn at a 45° angle. Cut through the layers of paper with a scalpel. Lift up the edges of the framing and peel off the surplus paper. Wipe the surface with a damp sponge. Leave to dry. Then varnish the box with at least three coats of matt acrylic varnish.

CHEST OF DRAWERS

This chest of drawers was perfect for decorating with a folk art design. When choosing a piece of furniture to decorate in this style, select one with simple lines, and without fussy detailing. This style of decoration would happily suit a larger set of drawers, but probably nothing smaller unless the scale of the decoration were reduced. Although the painted design is not an authentic representation of some of the wonderful folk art designs to have come out of North America, it does encapsulate the general ambience of that style of furniture. As traditional folk art designs often employed leaf motifs, I created a design which used broad oak and ivy leaves twisting around a central stem to form two deep vertical borders at each side of the chest.

Sketch your proposed border onto a piece of tracing paper, using the motif given on page 138, and joining pieces with sticky tape if necessary. Hold the outline against the furniture to gauge how this will look. If you feel confident to do so, draw in more leaves to extend the border to fit the furniture, if necessary. You may, however, prefer to enlarge the pattern given at the back of the book using the appropriate facility on a photocopier. Photocopy as many patterns as necessary to make up the required depth needed to fill your piece of furniture, and then join these together. Choose a background colour to suit your own decor, but bear in mind that the stronger, deeper colours will work best.

Junk chests of drawers like this can be found in many junk stores and are perfect for a folk art style of decoration.

TREATMENT

The strong red colour of the base coat was given a broken-colour treatment using a simple scumble glaze. The semi-translucent colour was applied over the dry base coat and was distressed roughly with the bristles of a brush; this effect is more pleasing than that of flat colour, and the technique is relatively quick and easy to accomplish. Other colours that could be used for the base coat are deep yellow ochre or burnt orange. Avoid using either blue or green as the contrast is not strong enough between the base and the leaf colours. Once the scumbled base coat was dry, the drawer unit was painted with the decorative twisting leaf pattern.

MATERIALS
- Dusky pink emulsion paint
- Plum emulsion paint
- Acrylic scumble glaze (see page 12)
- Foliage image (see page 138)
- Dark green emulsion paint
- Dark plum emulsion paint
- Black emulsion paint
- Green emulsion paint
- White emulsion paint
- Acrylic varnish

EQUIPMENT
- Household paintbrush, 12mm (½in) wide
- Jam jar
- Photocopier
- Carbon paper
- Masking tape
- Pencil
- Fine artist's brush
- Mixing palette or saucer
- Screwdriver

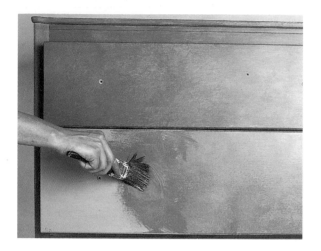

1 Paint the chest of drawers with a flat coat of dusky pink emulsion paint and leave to dry. Mix up the scumble glaze using equal quantities of plum emulsion paint and acrylic scumble glaze. Apply the scumble glaze over the chest by pushing it and gently scrubbing it into the surface with a brush. The pink base layer should be just visible through the plum brush marks.

2 Enlarge the foliage image to the right size using a photocopier. Place carbon paper underneath the enlarged image, then secure both to the chest of drawers with strips of masking tape; the dark, inky side of the carbon paper should face the wood. Draw over the lines with a pencil. Reverse the enlarged image and repeat on the other side of the chest.

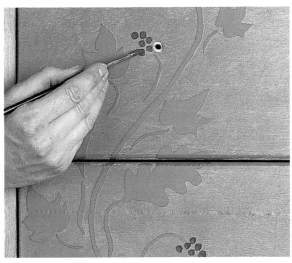

3 Using dark green emulsion paint and a fine artist's brush, paint the curvy stem. Use the same coloured paint to fill in the leaves, keeping the paint flat and even. Make sure that the edges of the leaves are neat. It is a good idea to start at the top left-hand corner of the image and gradually work down towards the right, to avoid smudging the paint.

4 Paint the berries individually with dark plum emulsion paint. When dry, mix a darker shade of plum by adding a little black emulsion paint. Paint a tiny spot of this colour onto each berry. Leave to dry.

5 Paint details on the leaves in two shades of green to look more realistic. Paint the dark green leaf veins first, to give shape to the leaf, then add the lighter green details. Keep the two kinds of leaf different: the oak leaf has both colours painted throughout, whereas the ivy has dark veins on the left and pale veins on the right, with a line around the edge.

6 Paint pale green highlights on the leaves to give the appearance of light catching the leaves. Always keep the end of the brush pointed when you paint these details to keep the leaves delicate. Leave the decoration to dry, then varnish with acrylic varnish. Replace the drawer knobs to complete the chest.

LINED DRESSING TABLE

This piece of junk furniture was a perfect find. As is the case with several of the pieces in this book, it had been abandoned and thrown away, literally 'junked'. It wasn't difficult to see why: an unsympathetic paint finish had been applied over the entire dressing table. The end result was several layers of thickly applied gloss paint and oil glaze. I suspect that the thought of having to strip the whole piece back to raw wood again was too daunting a task to contemplate, so out it went.

It is not unusual to find this type of badly painted furniture in junk shops and boot sales. Don't be put off by the surface appearance as paint, no matter how thickly applied, can always be removed. Instead, look at the shape of the piece itself. For me, the proportions of this dressing table were particularly attractive. The delicate, turned legs had a decidedly elegant appearance, and the arrangement of the four drawers – two small drawers on either side of the mirror and two wider drawers under the table top – were beautifully proportioned and created useful storage space. The mirror supports were rather wobbly but these could be fixed by tightening the screws on the hinges. I did notice a little wear and tear that was irreparable – some splitting of the veneer on the drawer fronts – but not enough to deter my enthusiasm at finding the piece and taking it home.

Despite its rundown appearance, I was struck by the elegant proportions and delicate turned legs of this dressing table. To make the most of these features I have given it a subtle paint and wax treatment, adding lining details to accentuate the furniture's fine shape.

TREATMENT

Once all the hard work of preparing and priming the dressing table had been completed (see pages 16–17), I was ready to begin painting. I had decided on a simple treatment of painting and lining, then a final rubbing over with furniture wax for an antiqued finish. When choosing your base colour for this technique, always bear in mind that the application of a coloured furniture wax will alter the final appearance.

The faded and antiqued duck-egg blue colour that now adorns this old dressing table started life as a swimming pool blue that was rather bright, yet if I had started using a colour close to the finished look the pigments in the wax would have masked the delicate tones. Although a professionally lined piece of furniture would be lined by hand using a specialist brush, for our purposes I suggest that masking tape is used for a similar effect. Using this method ensures that all the lines are perfectly even and, more important, perfectly straight.

The first thing to do is to determine where the lines will be and how narrow to

MATERIALS
- Dressing table
- Duck-egg blue emulsion paint
- Black acrylic paint
- Antiquing furniture wax

EQUIPMENT
- Household paintbrush, 2.5cm (1in) wide
- Steel ruler
- Pencil
- Low-tack masking tape
- Scissors
- Small jar
- Fine artist's brush
- Soft cotton cloth
- Medium-gauge wire wool

paint them. On this piece I kept the lining quite minimal to accentuate the pretty shape of the furniture, confining it to three sides of the table top, the top of the smaller drawers and the front of the two wider drawers.

1 Remove the drawers from the dressing table and work on these separately. Paint the dressing table and the drawers with a thin coat of duck-egg blue paint, working it well into any awkward angles. When dry, apply a second coat, then leave to dry again.

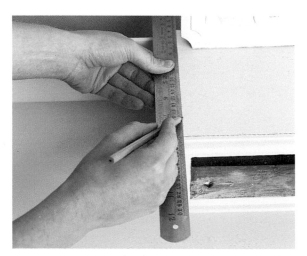

2 To line the three sides of the table top, the top of the smaller drawers and the front of the two wider drawers, mark the area to be lined. Using a steel ruler and pencil, measure and mark a line 6mm (¼in) in from the edge. Then mark a second line 6mm (¼in) in from this.

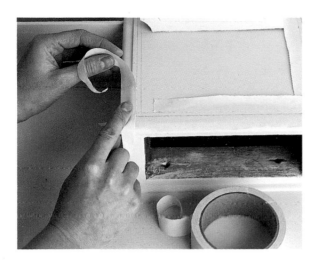

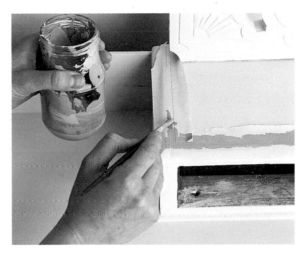

3 Stick low-tack masking tape along the pencilled lines to mask off the surrounding areas, leaving visible the area to be painted. To reduce the risk of lifting off any paint, stick down only the edge of the tape nearest to the pencil line and allow the rest of the tape to remain unstuck. For the perfect right angles, cut the tape into the corners.

4 To make the lining colour, mix up a little of the base colour paint with a squeeze of black acrylic paint in a small jar. Using a fine artist's brush, apply the paint between the lines of masking tape. Feather the paint inwards from both pieces of tape to prevent it being forced underneath the tape. Remove the tape carefully when you have completed an area.

5 When the lining is completely dry, start to apply the furniture wax. Load a soft cotton cloth with a generous amount of wax and rub this over a workable area of the furniture. You should use enough pressure to make your arm ache after a few minutes. Do not worry if some of the underlying colour comes off onto the surface of the cloth; this will enhance the final effect. However, if you start to see the natural colour of the wood showing through, rub less hard.

6 Rub a pad of medium-gauge wire wool over the surface using a circular, scrubbing motion. The aim is to enhance the antiqued finish further and to rub away some areas, as far down as the primed layer. Remove the paint entirely in some places, to reveal the natural wood around some edges and corners that naturally would have seen most wear and tear. Soften the lining gently with the wire wool to give it a distressed look. Allow the wax to build up in any nooks and crannies.

SEWING BOX

This charming sewing box was a rather shabby piece of furniture that had been cast aside at a local junk shop, alongside the equally disastrous-looking bathroom cabinet that was given the punched tin treatment (see page 104). I paid very little for both pieces and I think I was doing the vendor an enormous favour by taking them away. It can be fascinating and often rewarding to scour around at the back of junk shops; in these dusty corners I often unearth the really battered pieces of furniture and more unusual finds that are deemed unsaleable. These can be the most rewarding finds of all, as they are genuine pieces of junk for which people have given up any hope of a future.

I loved the simplicity of this sewing box, and it was perfect for a transformation. The basic structure was sound; there were no wobbly legs, broken sides or

splitting veneer, and even the hinge mechanism was in perfect working order – it was irresistible. I decided to cover the sewing box with fabric. Almost any printed cotton can be used for this type of decoration. This Toile de Jouy fabric with its picture motif fitted the bill perfectly as the central motif could be positioned on the front, sides and top of the unit. For covering furniture with shaped sides, you may prefer to cut out a paper template for each section first.

Although this unit could still be used as a sewing box it makes a rather attractive if slightly unusual bedside table. To prevent damage on the top of the unit, cover this with a piece of glass with safely ground edges.

TREATMENT

I had been searching for a piece of furniture that was suitable for covering in fabric and this sewing box fitted the bill in several ways. It had perfectly flat sides with no moulding or recessed panels, and a simple flat-fronted drawer. The legs were unfussy with no turned details and, importantly, these were flush with the main top part of the sewing box, which would make fabric-covering a good deal easier.

If I had chosen to paint the sewing box I would have had to undertake a considerable amount of preparation work. As it was, for the process of covering it with fabric the unit simply required a thorough sanding and a coat of acrylic-based primer. As the fabric I used has a pale cream base colour it was important to work over a pale surface; any dark areas would immediately show through the fabric and spoil the effect. One coat of primer should give you adequate coverage, but if dark patches still show through the layer of paint after one coat, apply subsequent coats until the coverage is even throughout.

I used a Toile de Jouy fabric to cover this sewing box, but other printed fabrics would work just as well. Choose a light cotton fabric, as this is easiest to work with and will not be too bulky at the corners or edges where it needs to be folded over for a neat finish. Silks, satins, gauzes or other delicate fabrics are not suitable for this project as they may mark badly when the PVA glue is applied.

MATERIALS
- Sewing box
- White acrylic primer
- Light cotton patterned fabric
- PVA glue
- Paper
- Hardboard
- Wadding material
- Plain cotton fabric
- Drawer knob and screw

EQUIPMENT
- Household paint-brush, 12mm (½in) wide
- Tape measure
- Pencil
- Sharp scissors
- Sharp craft knife
- Tenon saw
- Medium-grade sandpaper
- Screwdriver

1 Paint the sewing box with a coat of white acrylic primer and leave to dry. If patches of dark colour show through the primer, paint on more primer until the colour is even. Measure the dimensions of one leg of the sewing box and the length of the leg, allowing a 2.5cm (1in) overlap to tuck under the bottom. Transfer these measurements onto the wrong side of your chosen fabric, marking the fabric if necessary on the wrong side with a pencil.

2 Cut out the fabric for each leg of the box. Centre the printed design of the fabric accurately with the centre of each leg, taking into account that the overlap section should be positioned at the back of each leg where it will not be seen. Repeat for the remaining three legs, aligning the print where necessary.

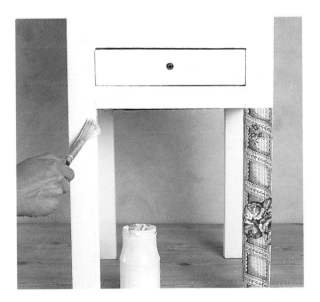

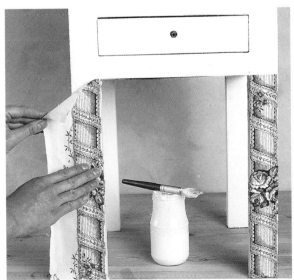

3 Apply a thin coat of PVA glue to all surfaces of each leg in turn. Carefully place the fabric in position over the glue, taking care to align the printed design by eye before allowing it to touch the adhesive.

4 When the fabric is positioned, press it down firmly with your fingertips, starting from the centre and moving outwards to avoid trapping air bubbles. A little extra glue may be needed on the overlap.

5 Remove the drawer and glue the front section in place. Cut out a hole for the drawer by making a slit across the centre of the fabric with sharp scissors; stop 5cm (2in) before the edges of the drawer. Then cut diagonally into each of the four corners from this centre point. Trim the overhanging edges of the fabric.

6 Glue the flaps down neatly inside the drawer opening, keeping these as flat as possible so that the drawer is easy to operate. Once the front has been completed, move around the sides of the sewing box.

7 Mark off the measurements with a tape measure, and position and glue the fabric over the sides of the box. Apply extra glue at the cut edges to prevent the fabric fraying.

8 Cover the lid of the box as before, gluing the overlaps neatly inside the lid. Hold the fabric firmly at each corner for a couple of seconds to achieve a neat, flat finish. Use extra glue on the cut edges to hold these securely and prevent fraying. Although milky when applied, the adhesive will dry to a clear finish.

9 Cover the drawer with one piece of fabric, selecting a piece that aligns with the fabric already in place on the front of the sewing box. Allow the fabric to dry overnight. If the drawer is difficult to slide in, trim away some of the excess material from the edges using a sharp craft knife.

10 To pad the inside of the sewing box lid, measure the area to be covered and cut a paper template of this area. Draw this shape onto a piece of hardboard and cut it out using a tenon saw. Smooth the rough edges with sandpaper. Cut out a piece of wadding using the template and glue this onto the hardboard.

11 Cut out a piece of plain fabric using the template as a guide and allowing an extra 2.5cm (1in) all around for turning. Glue this over the wadding; glue the allowance to the wrong side, and allow to dry.

12 Glue the padded section in place under the lid. Line the inside of the sewing box with the same contrasting fabric as that used for the box lid. Finally, screw a new drawer knob onto the sewing box drawer.

TRACE-OFF MOTIFS

Chest of drawers page 124

Mosaic table page 44

Stencilled cabinet page 40

Kitchen dresser page 92

Damask stencilled chair
page 90

Dressing-table set page 116

Gilded lamps page 62

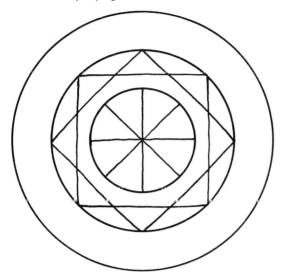

Stamped cupboard page 100

Punched tin cabinet page 104

SUPPLIERS

UK

TEXTILES

J. D. McDougall Ltd.
4 McGrath Road
London
E15 4JP
Tel: 0181 534 2921
*Canvas, hessian.
(Ring for appointment)*

Russell & Chapple Ltd.
23 Monmouth Street
Covent Garden
London
WC1 9DD
Tel: 0171 836 7521
Canvas, hessian. Art suppliers

PAINTS

J. W. Bollom
121 South Liberty Lane
Ashton Vale
Bristol
Tel: 01272 665151

Cornelissen & Son
105 Gt Russell Street
London
WC1B 3LX
Tel: 0171 636 1045

Dulux Decorative Paints
For details of product range and your nearest stockist contact:
ICI Paints
Wexham Road
Slough
Berkshire
SL2 5DS
Tel: 01753 550000

Foxell & James
57 Farringdon Road
London
EC1M 3JB
Tel: 0171 405 0152
Varnishes, stains, paints

Green & Stone
259 Kings Road
London
SW3
Tel: 0171 352 0837
Glazes, artist's materials

Nutshell Natural Paint
10 High Street
Totnes
Devon
TQ9 5RY
Tel: 01803 867770
Earth and mineral pigments. Natural paints, waxes

John Oliver Paints
33 Pembridge Road
London
W11 3HG
Tel: 0171 221 6466
Paint colours in own range, papers

Papers & Paints
4 Park Walk
London
SW10 0AD
Tel: 0171 352 8626
Paints, glazes

J. H. Ratcliffe & Co.
135a Linaker Street
Southport
PR8 5DF
Tel: 01704 537999
Scumble glazes, varnishes. (Mail order)

FOAM RUBBER

Pentonville Rubber
104/106 Pentonville Road
London
N1 9JB
Tel: 0171 837 4582

FABRIC COLOURS

London Graphic Centre
107/115 Long Acre
London
WC2E 9NT
Tel: 0171 240 0095
Fabric paints, art suppliers

GILDING

Green & Stone
(see address above)

Cornelissen & Son
(see address above)

MOSAICS

Edgar Udny & Co Ltd.
314 Balham High
Balham
London
SW17
Tel: 0181 767 8181

TIN (AND GILDING MATERIALS)

Alec Tiranti Ltd.
70 High Street
Theale
Reading
Berkshire
RG7 5AR
Tel: 0118 930 2775

or

27 Warren Street
London
W1P 5DG
Tel: 0171 636 8565

Australia

Handworks
121 Commercial Road
Prahan
Vic 3181
Tel: (03) 9820 8399

Hornsby Paint Warehouse
89 Hunter Street
Hornsby
NSW 2077
Tel: (02) 9477 7122

Janet's Art Supplies
143–145 Victoria Avenue
Chatswood
NSW 2067
Tel: (02) 9417 8572

The Painted Earth
6 Leura Street
Nedlands
WA 6009
Tel: (09) 389 8450

INDEX

ACKNOWLEDGEMENTS

A special thank you to all those people who were involved in the publication of this book.

To Lucinda Symons for her glorious photography and Jane Forster for her inspiring design work on the book.

Thanks also to Sally for her assistance in simply getting the job done.

Also to the two people who matter most of all, Chris and Jessica.